To
Helen Bagby Hopper
and
Stanley Romaine Hopper
My First and Finest Teachers

CONTENTS

ACKNOWLEDGMENTS

ALTHOUGH IT IS not possible to recognize, much less to acknowledge, all of the persons to whom one becomes indebted during a lifetime's education, there are many persons for whose assistance in the present work I would like to express my gratitude. There are, first of all, the many students who have labored with me at the Methodist Theological School in Ohio during the past quarter-century's efforts to enable theological thinking and understanding relevant to our time and place. They were the first to test seriously earlier versions of most of these chapters. Among the many colleagues and friends who have provided helpful advice I should particularly like to thank Dr. Everett Tilson, Professor of Old Testament, Dr. Sharon Ringe, Professor of New Testament, Dr. Robert Tannehill, Professor of New Testament (all of the Methodist Theological School), Dr. Tony Peterle, Professor of Biology at Ohio State University, and Dr. Leonard Russell, Professor of Physics at Ohio Wesleyan University. Each of these read drafts of the material contained herein which is in his or her area of specialization. Such errors and infelicities as remain are, of course, the responsibility of the author. My father, Stanley R. Hopper, read drafts of all of these chapters and made helpful suggestions, but my indebtedness to and gratitude for his teaching, example, and encouragement are far greater than anything that can be indicated here. I would like especially to express my gratitude to my wife, Jean, who, besides putting up with all that a project such as this entails and providing continuing encouragement, was the first to read the various drafts of all of the chapters and offer suggestions to enhance their clarity and readability. Without her support there would have been no book. I am grateful, too, for the advice, encouragement, and assistance given by Dr. John Hollar, Dr. Davis Perkins, Dr. Harold W. Rast, Stephanie Egnotovich, and Mimi McGinnis of Fortress Press.

INTRODUCTION

THE RIGHT-HAND WHEELS of a car driven by a newly licensed youth slip off the pavement. In anxious haste to regain full control and safety, the driver yanks the car to the left, loses control, and is carried into the path of an on-coming truck. Three teenagers die. The parents demand, "Why did God do this?" Or, "Why did God let this happen?" Or, "How can anyone believe there is a God when things like this happen?" These are first of all cries of anguish and not theological questions. They call for pastoral care, not learned discourses. Yet, they are also theological questions, and those who ask them in shock, anger, and anguish may and should still be asking them at later stages of the grief process and beyond.

That the first of these questions should be asked so often in our culture is a measure of the failure of Christian education. As an expression of parental shock, anger, and possibly guilt, the question is quite understandable. As an expression of understanding of Christian faith, it is quite impossible. God did not kill them.

The other questions are more difficult. There are answers, but they are not simple. In a situation like this, that difficulty is greatly increased by the paucity of previous thought and understanding which so many persons bring with them when they are confronted by such tragic events. Sadly, most people do not grapple with the most serious questions until confronted by life-shaking events. More sadly, some of the priests and pastors have offered those people very little real help, and a wide array of radio and TV preachers and "evangelists" are preying constantly upon their ignorance and anxieties with mind-numbing placebos. The word "placebo" is borrowed here from its medical use, meaning a medicine given merely to please the patient. (It is not without significance that medicine borrowed the word from a religious ritual!) The popular religious practice of telling people what they want to hear is

1

an encouragement to avoid the risk of faith by hiding in false securities, whether the "preacher" realizes this or not. For that very reason, such preaching will always be more widely welcomed than will serious theological efforts. Seen from its negative side, theology is "iconoclasm," the smashing of idols, where "idol" means anything *other than* God in which we place our basic trust. The smashing of others' idols has some popularity. The smashing of one's own is usually resisted with every means at one's disposal. This is one of the major reasons why there is so little understanding of modern theology. Most popular religion today is based—albeit superficially—upon premodern theologies, and most of it is idolatrous. It is one of the tasks of theology to reveal these facts, so it is hardly surprising that modern theologies are often branded "heretical." More than anything else, such charges are an indication of the great gulf that separates the popular and the premodern understandings of Christian faith from the teachings of the theologians who recognize that citizens of the developed nations today live in terms of a different basic world of experience than that of Christians of the eras in which the various orthodox theologies were formulated—and who seek therefore to reinterpret Christian faith for our understanding.

This book is an attempt to introduce "modern" theology to serious and thoughtful people. It seeks to lay a foundation for the answering of such questions as, "Why did God allow these young people to die?" But because those who are *beginning* serious study in theology usually have an understanding of Christian faith that is more influenced by premodern than modern theologies, the laying of that foundation must begin with an explication of the differences between premodern and modern theologies.

The word "modern" is being used here in the broad sense in which it designates the general characteristics of societies that have been profoundly influenced by cultural revolutions whose impact began in the seventeenth century. Some authors speak today of "the post-modern mind" (Smith 1982) or of "postmodern theologies" (Taylor 1984). When these distinctions are made, they limit "modern" to certain characteristics of the seventeenth, eighteenth, and nineteenth centuries in the Western world that may be described as "scientific," "empiricistic," and "naturalistic," characteristics that exclude meaning and faith. Such a distinction serves purposes differing from those of this study, where "modern" is used in the more common sense and *includes* what such authors call "postmodern."

The approach followed in this volume is historical. The differences developed gradually along with and largely as a result of other cultural revolutions. It is likely that anyone who reads this book will be familiar with the names and achievements of Copernicus, Galileo, Descartes, Newton, Kant, Darwin, Einstein, Freud, and other thinkers who contributed to the character of the world in which we live, but few today seem to have undertaken the task of considering carefully the possible implications of these thinkers' collective cultural impact for the understanding of Christian faith. The following chapters review the cultural revolutions associated with these names with specific attention to the basic theological questions that were implicit in their most influential conclusions. The final chapter introduces a "revolution" that bridges the gap between the scientific revolutions (both natural and social) examined in the first four chapters and the area of theology itself, the development of modern biblical scholarship. The acceptance or nonacceptance of historical-critical approaches to the Scriptures is the most obvious point of contrast between modern and premodern theologies and would appear to be the most divisive issue within Christendom today. Unfortunately the usual rejections of modern biblical scholarship are not based upon understanding of its origins, nature, or implications.

Historical-critical studies of the Scriptures are not yet modern theology, however, though they are intimately related thereto. They pose, in fact, the same basic theological questions that are raised by these other cultural revolutions, reflecting the general characteristics of the "modern world." When the challenges posed to Christian theology by the development of this modern world have been clarified it will be possible to introduce the general characteristics of modern theology. That is the aim of a subsequent volume.

WORKS CITED

Smith, H.
    1982   *Beyond the Post-Modern Mind*. New York: Crossroad.
Taylor, M. C.
    1984   *Erring: A Postmodern, A-Theology*. Chicago: University of Chicago Press.

1

A NEW WORLD

The Impact of the Beginnings of Modern Science

"IN THE BEGINNING God created the heavens and the earth. . . ." "I believe in God the Father almighty, maker of heaven and earth." These familiar words from Genesis and from the Apostles' Creed remain a basic part of the affirmation of Christian theology today. Yet while this might be offered as evidence of a remarkable continuity of Christian affirmation over many centuries, it would be extremely difficult to defend the thesis that those statements carry the same meaning today as they did for the generations who lived before the scientific revolution of the seventeenth century. The century in which appeared the works of Bacon, Harvey, Kepler, Galileo, Huygens, and Newton, as well as of Descartes, Pascal, Locke, Spinoza, and Leibniz stands between us and the "world" not only of Augustine and Aquinas, but also that of Luther and Calvin. Inevitably, our words and ideas carry different assumptions.

In order to begin to grasp the magnitude of the change in perspective, it is necessary to comprehend something of the common understanding of the world that preceded the development of "modern" science. The measure of our difficulty in taking seriously some of the beliefs that were then held so strongly is but a clue to the difficulty that people had in breaking loose from those long-cherished convictions.

This "common understanding" of the cosmos was never a matter of complete agreement in all particulars nor of the simple acceptance of any one person's theories and interpretations. There were variations, suggestions, and disagreements. Nevertheless, a common basic perspective was present in medieval Christendom. It was derived from various sources including the teachings of Aristotle, Ptolemy (2d century c.e.), and the Bible. The earth was firmly believed to be at the center of the cosmos, and it was equally firmly believed to be at rest there. In Aristotle's interpretation, the earth was not simply the central point around which the planets and stars moved, but was the center of a series of concentric spheres. What have come to be called the "fixed stars" were understood to be carried about by an outer shell of the universe, and between that sphere and the earth there were at least fifty-three other spheres, the large number being needed to account for the apparent movements of the planets. Such an interpretation was partly the result of the conviction that there could not be a void or empty space, and also of the understanding of motion.

Our difficulty in finding anything seriously believable in the Aristotelian doctrine of spheres (which in complex ways fill all the "space" of the universe and account mechanically for the movements of the stars, the planets, the sun, and the moon) is a good illustration of the fact that we do not experience things simply in terms of what we see but also in terms of what we have been taught. The idea that it is natural for things to be at rest and that it is motion that must always be explained is certainly an obvious inference from common human experience. But we have been taught to believe in "inertia" —an object in motion will continue that motion except insofar as various factors may modify or impede that motion. The observation of new data concerning the moon and the planets opened the way for this hypothesis, but it was a very difficult idea to develop after so many centuries of another assumption.

There were serious difficulties with the interpretation of motion that underlay Aristotle's description of the cosmos. It included the belief that an object would continue in motion only as long as the "mover," the cause of its motion, was in contact with it. Taken strictly, this should mean that an arrow would fall to the ground as soon as contact with the bowstring was broken. But an explanation was developed in which the air was said to move continually in behind the moving object in such fashion as to push it along. That such a theory should have persisted in spite of its rather obvious difficulties is but another indication of the degree to which we are the victims of our assumptions.

These beliefs about motion were important in relation to the movements of the planets and the stars. Why, for example, did they not fall to the earth? For some this might be accounted for by their not being freely moving bodies but, rather, contained within their spheres. In addition, it was believed that they were made of a special "higher" element. They were basically better in kind, higher in the scale of being. This is also why they were believed to move in circular paths—the circle and sphere being believed to be "perfect" movements—and further explains why they were believed to be smooth. Clearly then there were many metaphysical doctrines mixed in with various rather obvious interpretations of natural appearances. For us the idea that a "heavenly body" is moved by a higher "intelligence" is, to put it mildly, extremely odd. But in the thirteenth century, for example, it was something of a culmination of the observations and the wisdom of the centuries that is reflected in the following lines from Saint Thomas Aquinas:

> A proof that the heavenly bodies are moved by the direct influence and contact of some spiritual substance, and not by nature, like heavy and light bodies, lies in the fact that whereas nature moves to one fixed end, in which having attained it, it rests; this does not appear in the movement of heavenly bodies. Hence it follows that they are moved by some intellectual substances. (Aquinas 1945, 1:660)

Before turning to the teachings of medieval scholars and the importance of Christian beliefs therein, however, it will be useful to note certain differences between Aristotle's explanations and those of Ptolemy. The latter was not a philosopher trying to explain the various aspects of human experience in terms of a basic interpretation of reality as a whole, but an astronomer trying to account for the observed motions of the stars and the planets. He, too, accepted the assumption that the earth is at the center.

That is, after all, a very natural assumption. Until very recently it was the point from which we made all of our observations of the universe. It certainly appears that the moon, sun, planets, and stars move around us. Indeed, there is a sense in which they do. It is also quite natural to assume that the earth is at rest. Our experience of rapid motion has shown us that it involves increasing resistance from the air as the speed of the movement increases. The speed of rotation of the earth on its axis, for example, which is required to account for the appearance of the motions of sun and stars would naturally be assumed to entail an utterly unimaginable force of wind, which, however, we do not experience. When such theorizers as Aristarchus (310–230 B.C.E.) and Nicholas of Oresme (fourteenth century C.E.) argued that the earth moves, the additional theories that were to account for the absence of this enormous wind resistance were not available, and this rather natural basis of the denial of the earth's movement was still being used in the time of Galileo.

But this assumption was not without difficulties. Careful observations even by the naked eye reveal that the planets do not always maintain a simple circular movement around the earth. As Aristotle put it, "That the movements are more numerous than the bodies that are moved is evident to those who have given even moderate attention to the matter; for each of the planets has more than one movement" (Aristotle 1941, 882). In relation to the fixed stars a planet will at times appear to stop its movement, then move backward, stop again, and resume its original course. Aristotle used and modified a theory of concentric spheres developed by Eudoxus and Callippus as a means of accounting for these appearances while maintaining the centrality of the earth. It was this need for several spheres to account for the movement of each planet that necessitated the large number of spheres in his above-noted cosmology. This theory was not, then, a simple explanation of the movements of the planets, but it did preserve the central position of the earth and the concept of the perfect spheres that the philosophical convictions required.

In the theory that came to be known primarily through the writings of Claudius Ptolemy these spheres were done away with, and more data was explained in a simpler hypothesis. Changes in the speed and in the brightness of the planets as well as the changes in direction were accounted for by a theory of cycles and epicycles. In this view it remains true that the planets move around the earth on circular paths, but they are not simple circular paths. As a planet moves around the earth it is also continually moving through a series of smaller circular orbits; it is, therefore, this continual series of orbits that moves on the larger circular path around the earth (Ptolemy 1948, 13).

Given the assumptions that we take for granted today, such a theory seems incredible, but that is just one illustration of the fact that the assumptions of the centuries before Galileo were vastly different from those that have developed since. The centrality of the sun had been proposed and rejected. The means of making certain basic observations were not available. This theory not only explained the available data while maintaining the centrality of the earth and the convictions concerning the perfection of circular movements and spherical shapes, but it also made possible the preparation of tables from which the positions of the sun, the moon, and the planets—and thus also eclipses—could be predicted for any future dates.

To this impressive evidence and the obvious natural assumptions about the centrality of the earth must be added the testimony of Scripture and the general impact of Christian teaching. Of course, the Bible does not write of nested spheres or of cycles and epicycles, it does not proclaim the perfection of circular movements or the finitude of the universe and the impossibility of a void, nor does it specifically assert that the earth is the center of the universe. Nevertheless, these writings, which were believed throughout Christendom to speak with the authority of God, did reflect the assumption of the centrality of the earth, and it was a matter of Christian conviction that the whole creation existed for the sake of the drama of salvation between God and humanity. The first chapter of Genesis is easily heard in terms of those interpretations. Probably the most famous passage in this connection comes from the tenth chapter of Joshua:

Then spoke Joshua to the Lord in the day when the Lord gave the Amorites over to the men of Israel; and he said in the sight of Israel,

"Sun, stand thou still at Gibeon,
and thou Moon in the valley of Aijalon."
And the sun stood still, and the moon stayed,
until the nation took vengeance on their enemies.

Is this not written in the Book of Jashar? The sun stayed in the midst of heaven, and did not hasten to go down for about a whole day. There has been no day like it before or since, when the Lord hearkened to the voice of a man; for the Lord fought for Israel. (Josh. 10:12–14, RSV)

Other passages often cited include (all RSV): Ps. 93:1 ("Yea, the world is established; it shall never be moved . . ."); Ps. 104:5 ("Thou didst set the earth on its foundations, so that it should never be shaken"); Eccles. 1:5 ("The sun rises and the sun goes down, and hastens to the place where it rises").

Thus when the issue was raised critically by Galileo, there was a long-established conviction supported by the apparent convergence of natural assumptions, science, philosophy, and Holy Scripture. The importance of this fact lies primarily in the recognition that the challenge focused in Galileo was not concerned most basically with the question of the relative movements of earth and sun and planets, but rather with the question of just how one should go about answering such questions.

That the questions of method and authority were the more important concerns can be seen by a comparison of the bases upon which Nicholas of Cusa, Nicholas Copernicus, and Galileo Galilei each defended a new interpretation of the universe.

Nicholas of Cusa (Nicolaus Cusanus, 1401–64), papal legate and cardinal, denied that the earth is the center of the universe and that it is without motion. These denials were not, however, a matter of astronomy but of philosophy and theology. They were aspects of a particular interpretation of the infinity of God that had implications for the understanding of the nature of the universe and the limitations of human knowledge. Because of this philosophical-theological concern, the accepted doctrines of the finitude of the universe with the earth at its center and of the hierarchy of being in that universe according to which the earth was inferior to the other bodies therein were rejected. It was affirmed that God was both the center and the circumference of the whole creation, that the various bodies in the universe could not be said to move in perfect circular paths, that the earth also moved, that any description of these movements depended upon the particular point from which one observed them, and so forth (Cusanus 1954, Bk. II). The details and the subtleties need not concern us here. What is to be noted is that this rather thorough rejection of the accepted medieval understanding of the universe and the associated philosophical and theological doctrines was still an example of the generally accepted methods of reasoning. Its hypotheses were rather easily put aside.

In the work of Nicholas Copernicus (1473–1543) we are dealing with something very different. The focus of his (eventually) epoch-making work, *On the Revolutions of the Heavenly Spheres*, was on the understanding of the cosmos. The basic argument was the presentation of a simpler mathematical scheme than that of Ptolemy for accounting for the apparent movements of the sun, moon, planets, and stars. That is, the central concerns here were not philosophy and theology but astronomy and mathematics.

At the same time it must be noted that this contrast can easily be overstated. The very conviction that a simpler explanation was a preferable one, a view shared by Ptolemy, is a philosophical belief of the Pythagorean-Platonic tradition. Copernicus was influenced during his studies at Bologna by the Platonist Domenico di Novara. J. J. Langford has suggested that "it was probably Novara who convinced Copernicus that the Ptolemaic system was far too complex to satisfy the principle of mathematical harmony and that there must be a simpler way to 'save the appearances'" (Langford 1966, 33). Copernicus's own account describes his examination of all the philosophical works he could obtain, seeking for some better explanation, and states that it was first in Cicero and then in Plutarch that he found references to theories according to which the earth moves (Copernicus 1939, 508). Further, Alexandre Koyré points out that one of the reasons Copernicus gave for the preferability of the theory of the earth's movement was that it is nobler and more divine for a body to be at rest than to be subject to change. And Koyré also notes that one of the reasons given for the central position of the sun was precisely its higher dignity. Both of these arguments, while opposing the accepted beliefs about the relative status of earth and sun, are nevertheless very much in keeping with the medieval perspective (Koyré 1957, 30).

Nevertheless, while these and other points can be offered to show the importance of the philosophical factors in the development of the Copernican hypotheses, one should not ignore the importance of his studies of astronomy based on years of observations and of labor over geometrical charts of the heavens. It was these labors that produced his new depiction of the universe in which the earth and the planets move around the sun, an interpretation that, while considerably simpler than the Ptolemaic model, offered a comparable accuracy in terms of the available observations.

Langford has drawn attention to two often-ignored facts regarding the reception of Copernicus's theory. The first is that in 1533 Pope Clement II arranged for a public lecture to be given at the Vatican to explain the theory whose outline Copernicus had circulated in 1530. The response by the pope was favorable, and Copernicus was urged by Nicholas Cardinal Schoenberg to arrange for the publication of the full details. The second fact is that Copernicus resisted this urging not because of a fear of persecution, but of ridicule. As he put it, "... the scorn which I had to fear on account of the newness and absurdity of my opinion almost drove me to abandon a work already undertaken" (Langford 1966, 35). As evidence that Copernicus had indeed reason to fear such scorn, Langford quotes the famous statement attributed to Martin Luther:

> People give ear to an upstart astrologer who strove to show that the earth revolves, not the heavens or the firmament, the sun and the moon. Whosoever wishes to appear clever must devise some new system which of all systems, of course, is the very best. This fool wishes to reverse the entire science of astronomy; but Sacred Scripture tells us that Josue commanded the sun to stand still, and not the earth. (Ibid.)

While there is some question whether Luther actually said this, it would hardly be surprising or to his discredit if he did. We seem sometimes to suppose today that a sun-centered universe is obviously to be preferred to an earth-centered universe and that once this was pointed out it should have been readily accepted. Such a supposition ignores several considerations. To begin with, no description of the universe worth mentioning is either simple or obvious. Anyone who will take the trouble even to leaf through Ptolemy's *The Almagest* and Copernicus's *On the Revolutions of the Heavenly Spheres* will soon recognize the immense complexity of the observations and calculations involved in each. Neither of these works offers what today would be called "proof," however. Rather, each offers an interpretation of basically the same appearances. Each does so partly on the basis of assumptions "foreign" to us. And neither of those theories fully accounts for the observations that had been made. More than a hundred years after the death of Copernicus a student of astronomy had at least four different interpretations of the universe from which to choose (Butterfield 1957, chap. 4). When these factors are noted together with the long-standing convergence of the teachings of science, philosophy, and religion, it is not difficult to understand why Copernicus anticipated and received ridicule. After summarizing the various impediments to the acceptance of the new theory, E. A. Burtt argued,

> In the light of these considerations it is safe to say that even had there been no religious scruples whatever against Copernican astronomy, sensible men all over Europe, especially the most empirically minded, would have pronounced it a wild appeal to accept the premature fruits of an uncontrolled imagination, in preference to the solid inductions, built up gradually through the ages, of men's

confirmed sense experience. In the strong stress on empiricism, so characteristic of present-day philosophy, it is well to remind ourselves of this fact. Contemporary empiricists, had they lived in the sixteenth century, would have been first to scoff out of court the new philosophy of the universe. (Burtt 1932, 25)

Copernicus's work was then both far from an instance of "modern science" and at the same time so different from the beliefs of his own time as to seem absurd. These two observations when taken together are a first indication of the scope of the change wrought in our common beliefs and assumptions by the scientific revolution.

Copernicus is generally regarded as a forerunner of that revolution rather than an example of it. His interpretation of the universe was both important and revolutionary, but his method was not new. The reverence for mathematical harmony and simplicity was a characteristic of the Neoplatonic revival of the fifteenth century, and it should not be surprising that for some time his principal support was philosophical in character. Or, as Burtt put it, "Now during the half century after Copernicus, no one was bold enough to champion his theory save a few eminent mathematicians like Rheticus and a few incorrigible intellectual radicals like Bruno" (ibid., 44).

The most significant astronomer of that half century was Tycho Brahe (1546–1601), who offered much more than Copernicus had by way of new observational knowledge, and who proposed another explanation of the relative positions and motions of the earth and the "heavenly bodies." In this theory the immobility of the earth is retained, but the planets revolve around the sun which moves around the earth. In his correspondence with Galileo, he also argued against the Copernican theory on the basis of the empirical evidence of his careful observations that showed no change in the relative positions of the stars—which should be found if indeed the earth moved as Copernicus argued. Very simply, if the point from which one observes two or more stationary objects changes, then the relative positions of those stationary objects will appear to be different. According to the Copernican theory the position of the earth differed every six months by 186 million miles, and the lack of any observable change in the relative positions of the stars seemed accordingly to be serious evidence against that theory. The distance which would be required to account for that lack of observable change was far too great to be taken seriously at that time. It was not until the 1830s that Thomas Henderson, Friedrich Wilhelm Bessel, and Friedrich Georg Wilhelm von Struve made the observations that refuted Brahe's argument.

The significance of Brahe's system has been explained by T. S. Kuhn:

The remarkable and historically significant feature of the Tychonic system is its adequacy as a compromise solution of the problems raised by *De Revolutionibus*.

Since the earth is stationary and at the center, all the main arguments against Copernicus' proposal vanish. Scripture, the laws of motion, and the absence of stellar parallax, all are reconciled by Brahe's proposal, and this reconciliation is effected without sacrificing any of Copernicus' major mathematical harmonies. The Tychonic system is, in fact, precisely equivalent mathematically to Copernicus' system. . . . It retained the mathematical advantages of Copernicus' system without the physical, cosmological, and theological drawbacks. (Kuhn 1959, 202, 205)

It is hardly surprising that scholars of the Roman College in Galileo's time tended to support Brahe's system rather than the traditional one Galileo was attacking, and it provided a part of the basis upon which the church could ask Galileo to treat the Copernican system as but a hypothesis.

The great emphasis upon observation in Brahe should not, however, lead one too hastily to place him among modern empiricists. In addition to being an astronomer he was also an astrologer. The same may be said of Johann Kepler (1571–1630) who worked with Brahe and inherited both his position and the records of his observations. Kepler became persuaded of the Copernican theory while in the course of studies for the ministry. He was persuaded because he shared the reverence for mathematical harmony. While yet a student he attempted to reconcile the Copernican theory with the teachings of Scripture, and not long after he reluctantly accepted a position as an astronomer he wrote that "God in creating the universe and regulating the course of the cosmos had in view the five regular bodies of geometry as known since the days of Pythagoras and Plato" (Kepler 1939, 841). This is still not what today is called "science."

Nevertheless, Kepler produced interpretations of the available observations that proved to be of the greatest significance. Best known of these "discoveries" is that of the elliptical orbits of the planets. Here again, the role of religious-philosophical conviction is of great importance. Kepler's great devotion to the mathematical perfection of the universe provided the motivation for his work and guided the formulation of his hypotheses. But unlike many of his time it did not lead him to ignore or try to explain away embarrassing data. Quite the contrary. Because of that devotion he had to find adequate description and explanation. He could give up a hallowed conviction (such as the presumed circular motions) and search for a new understanding because of the firm belief that what he would find would necessarily be an expression of the mathematical perfection given by the ultimate cause, the Unmoved Mover-God. The authority given here to observation and the willingness to surrender old doctrines and formulate new hypotheses in terms of the observations point toward the developing science. The religious devotion that underlies it does not.

It is in Galileo Galilei (1564–1642) that the decisive characteristics of modern science are usually judged first to have been brought together. As W. C. Dampier put it, "In a very real sense Galileo is the first of the moderns; as we read his writings, we instinctively feel at home; we know that we have reached the method of physical science which is still in use" (Dampier 1966, 129). Note that here again the focus is upon *method*. Galileo's importance lies more in the way in which he reached his conclusions than in those conclusions themselves. We shall therefore note some of those findings and then examine the method. It will then be useful to consider Galileo's struggle with the church.

It is a matter of "common knowledge" that Galileo employed the telescope to provide empirical evidence proving Copernicus's theory that it is the sun and not the earth that is the center of the universe and that Galileo as an old man was forced under threat of torture to abjure these teachings that he knew to be true. "Common knowledge" is not, however, to be trusted, and it is important to recognize how much is true and how much is untrue in this statement.

Galileo did improve and employ the recently invented telescope, and he made discoveries with it that did much to support the Copernican theory and to discredit certain traditional Aristotelian doctrines. He began his telescopic studies of the night skies in 1609, and in March of 1610 he published a pamphlet entitled *The Starry Messenger* in which he announced discoveries and interpretations that quickly made him both famous and controversial. After explaining how he had developed the telescope to the point that one could see objects almost a thousand times larger and more than thirty times closer than they are seen by the naked eye, he announced that his examinations of the moon had revealed a great many spots all over its surface. Repeated observations of these spots led him to the conclusion that the surface of the moon is not smooth and spherical but very much like the surface of the earth including mountains and valleys (Galileo 1957, 31).

Such an announcement sounds very commonplace to people who have not only been taught this since childhood but have sat in their homes and watched television pictures of men walking over the uneven surfaces of the moon. Galileo's age, however, was one in which it was believed that the moon was a "heavenly body" made of a fifth element (more perfect than the earth, air, fire, and water that were believed to be the elements from which all the material of our earthly experience was composed), and therefore incorruptible, smooth-surfaced, and spherical. It is easy today to say that since it had been seen that these beliefs were in error they should simply have been corrected. But this was no simple correction of a few facts. A whole way of experiencing the universe—and thus, indeed, all of life—was involved here and with it a whole way of determining the truth.

Perhaps the "system" could have been adjusted to accommodate these observations of the moon, but there was much more. Galileo announced that with the aid of the telescope one could see stars that had never before been seen, so many in fact that their number exceeded the total of all that had previously been known (ibid., 47). Further, he announced the solution to the ancient question concerning the nature of the Milky Way, declaring that with the help of the telescope he had been able to see that it was made up of clusters of innumerable stars (ibid., 49). What had previously been thought to be denser parts of the ether were also proclaimed to be clusters of stars (ibid., 50). Then Galileo came to the announcement that he believed to be of the greatest importance, his discovery of four new planets, referring to what we now call the satellites of Jupiter. He described and diagramed his conclusions, and then pointed out how this answered one of the arguments against Copernicus. That argument was that it did not make sense to have all of the planets circling around the sun except for the one peculiar instance of the moon circling the earth. The most immediate evidence for the Ptolemaic theory of the earth's centrality was this unexplained oddity in the Copernican theory. But now Galileo announced another case of such "moons." Our moon was no longer a unique case, and planetary satellites had to be accounted for in either theory (ibid., 57).

In this same document Galileo announced that he would subsequently prove that the earth moves and is essentially superior to the moon rather than "the sink of all dull refuse of the universe; . . ." (ibid., 45).

Galileo's announcements created a sensation, but they were far from universally accepted. James Brodrick quotes a writer named Christmann:

> We are not to think that Jupiter has four satellites given him by nature in order, by revolving round him, to immortalize the name of Medici. These are dreams of idle men, who love ludicrous ideas better than our laborious correction of the heavens. Nature abhors so horrible a chaos and to the truly wise such vanity is detestable. (Brodrick 1964, 41)

It is well to recall that very few people had ever seen or heard of a telescope, and it was far easier to doubt than to believe Galileo's claims. It seems that Stillman Drake was partly ignoring the importance of historical contexts when he wrote that "the arguments that were brought forward against the new discoveries were so silly that it is hard for the modern mind to take them seriously" (Galileo 1957, 73). "Hard for the modern mind" indeed, but Galileo was one of the geniuses whose work has led to "the modern mind," and arguments that seem silly today were not at all silly in the early seventeenth century. One of Drake's illustrations was the suggestion of Lodovico delle Colombe that though the surface of the moon appeared to be rough, it was covered by a smooth and invisible or transparent surface. That seems more than silly today, and it received Galileo's scorn. But Galileo, who had rejected Aristotelianism and espoused the Copernican theory long before he made his telescopic observations, could hardly be regarded as typical. The idea of invisible spheres in the heavens was an ancient and hallowed one, and it remains true in this day of our much-vaunted "modern minds" that most of us will grasp at any suggestion that will apparently allow us to continue holding those beliefs related to our security. What is remarkable is not that such arguments were offered, but that Galileo received considerable support from high officials of the church of Rome.

Thus far we have referred to only one aspect of Galileo's revolutionary scientific work, possibly not the most important one. Dampier argues that "Galileo's chief and most original work was the foundation of the science of dynamics" (Dampier 1966, 130). Earlier mention was made of the importance of the problem of motion and the (to us) very peculiar beliefs so long held on the subject. Galileo's work in this area, which was so important for his interpretation of the universe, clearly shows those factors in his methods that have often been labeled the real beginnings of modern science.

On the one hand, as Dampier emphasizes, Galileo no longer asked *why* things moved as they did, but *how*. That is, he was not dealing with metaphysics, either deducing explanations from it or trying to arrive at ultimate causes (ibid.). And, as Ian Barbour has argued, "The key feature in the new science was the combination of mathematical reasoning and experimental observation" (Barbour 1966, 23). For example, it had commonly been thought that the heavier an object is, the faster it will fall. Explanation was related to the metaphysical theory of a hierarchy of being in which the elements differed in their relative dignity or baseness. Galileo did not concern himself with such *explanations*, but with *description* in mathematical terms through experiment and observation.

His description of the discovery of the equations of accelerated motion, using a ball rolling down an inclined plane, is a classic example of the combination of induction and deduction, reasoning back and forth between theory and experiment. He used concepts such as length, time, and velocity which could be tied to measurements and expressed in mathematical symbols. He described how he considered a possible mathematical relationship between velocity and distance and then deduced the expected law this would yield—a deduction which turned out to be incompatible with experimental results. He tried other theoretical assumptions, calculated the equations deducible from them, and made experimental tests of these equations. Here were all the characteristics of the new science:

the distinctive type of concept, the combination of theory and experiment, and the goal of expressing laws of nature as mathematical relationships among measurable variables. (Ibid., 25)

Barbour goes on to underline the importance of imaginative new concepts here (as distinguished from the view that would see science simply in terms of observation and generalization) by reference to Galileo's idea of motion without resistance. This idea, which was necessary for the development of the concept of inertia, could not be based on any actual experience or observation. It had long been believed that things left to themselves would come to rest. Recall the use of this assumption in the quotation from Saint Thomas Aquinas above (p. 7). It had long seemed "self-evident," for that is, after all, what we continually experience. But Galileo "imagined observed motion to be the resultant of two abstractions, neither of which could be observed alone: a continuing uniform inertial motion and a frictional retarding force" (Barbour 1966, 25). Observation, imaginative hypotheses, experimentation, and mathematical description were the basic factors in the new approach. Insofar as possible, metaphysics and theology were avoided. But the impact of the new approach on metaphysics and theology was bound to be considerable simply because they *had been* closely bound up with the understanding of the same phenomena for so many centuries. Traditional metaphysics and theology were being displaced by the new methods of reaching understanding of the world, and they were being brought into question by the denial of their teachings. In this case Galileo's teachings concerning the universe and concerning motion were making the earth, occurrences on the earth, and the "heavenly bodies" all subject to the same laws and mathematical descriptions. The sun, moon, planets, and stars were being deprived of their mystery and divinity, and the philosophers were being questioned and restricted in their authority.

One might be tempted to question this last statement on the basis of the familiar contemporary claim that there can be no real conflict between science and theology because theology deals with the "transcendent," the "supernatural," and the "infinite," whereas science is concerned with the "finite," the "observable," and the "measurable." Whatever one's judgment may be about that contrast, it is important to notice here that it is the kind of distinction that the work of Galileo and others *led to*. It is a result of the change wrought by the development of science. In Galileo's time it was not a generally accepted way of thinking. It was, in fact, a most unusual way of thinking. This is evident not only in the considerable opposition to Galileo's teachings and in the contrast of his methods with those of Copernicus and Kepler, but also in certain of Galileo's own beliefs. He assumed throughout the controversy that the Scriptures are inerrant and that their teachings are in full accord with the valid findings of science. This assumption of the God-given perfection of Scripture was itself brought into serious question both directly and indirectly by the developing impact of the science Galileo was inaugurating.

Nevertheless, Galileo was a loyal member of the Roman Catholic Church, and he had no desire to call into question either its authority or that of the Scriptures. It seemed clear to him that it was not he but his opponents who were undermining the Bible's authority. He wrote,

> they go about invoking the Bible, which they would have minister to their deceit-ful purposes. Contrary to the sense of the Bible and the intention of the holy Fa-thers, . . . they would extend such authorities until even in purely physical matters—where faith is not involved—they would have us altogether abandon reason and the evidence of our senses in favor of some biblical passage, though under the surface meaning of its words this passage may contain a different sense. (Galileo 1957, 179).

This kind of argument had considerable plausibility. The Roman Catholic Church was never committed to biblical literalism, so one of the questions that always had to be faced in interpreting Scripture was concerned with the sense in which a passage should be understood. The literal was but one among several possibilities. In addition, the idea of "accommodation"—ac-cording to which the expressions in a particular biblical passage might be un-derstood to be an accommodation made to the ways of understanding of a particular time—had long been an accepted way of dealing with some pas-sages. For support of these arguments Galileo appealed even to Aquinas, spe-cifically on this doctrine of accommodation (ibid., 201). He could also have cited Aquinas's support of this doctrine from his discussion of the Genesis ac-count of creation wherein many of the beliefs concerning the cosmos Galileo was attacking were affirmed. Aquinas at several points held that certain pas-sages should be understood in terms of Moses' speaking to ignorant people and making allowance for their weakness in the way he expressed things (Aquinas 1945, 1:643). In the same general context Aquinas wrote,

> In discussing questions of this kind two rules are to be observed, as Augustine teaches. The first is, to hold the truth of Scripture without wavering. The second is that, since Holy Scripture can be explained in a multiplicity of senses, one should adhere to a particular explanation only in such measure as to be ready to abandon it, if it be proved with certainty to be false; lest Holy Scripture be ex-posed to the ridicule of unbelievers, and obstacles be placed to their believing. (Ibid., 637–38)

This was Galileo's argument, but that hardly settled the matter. Rather, in raising the very important question of *how* passages of the Bible should be interpreted, such arguments from an astronomer and mathematician were also raising the question of *who* should interpret the Bible. *Who* is to decide when evidence is sufficient to require the surrendering of a long-accepted interpretation? *Who* is to decide what other sense should be found in the passage? It may be clear to us that Galileo was eminently qualified to judge the evidence concerning certain issues in astronomy, but the prerogative of interpreting the Bible belonged to the church, and its theologians were jealous of that prerogative. Further, the struggles between Protestants and Catholics had done nothing to lessen sensitivity on this issue! Even so, Galileo was bold enough to proclaim how these questions should be settled. He argued that the Bible condescends to human capacities to understand even by attributing to God characteristics alien to the divine essence, showing that the Scriptures are not properly understood in every passage by rigid adherence to the restricted meanings of its words. Further, he contended, in physical matters we should not begin with the authority of scriptural passages but from observation and experiment, for nature, which also is a product of God's Word, is inexorably bound to the laws imposed on it by God, and its manifestations should not therefore be contradicted by reference to biblical passages that may have more than one possible interpretation (Galileo 1957, 182–83).

In theory at least the Roman Catholic theologians were in a better position to accept this kind of argument than were the Protestants, for Protestant Scholasticism with its doctrine of literal inerrancy and its view of the Bible as a book of information—including scientific information—reached its fullest expression precisely at the time when Kepler and Galileo first produced significant evidence for the Copernican theory. The doctrine of accommodation, employed by Calvin, was rejected by Protestant Scholasticism. But the foregoing argument by Galileo was bound to encounter serious opposition from Catholic theologians as well, for it not only constituted an invasion of their territory, but it rather clearly pointed to a displacement of the authority of both church and Scripture. Thus, however important one may judge such factors as rigid dogmatism, prejudice, ignorance, personal animosity, and politics to have been in Galileo's struggles with the Inquisition, it remains more significant in the long run that those churchmen who sensed here a "shaking of the foundations" were correct. The church still had the power in some places to call scientists to account for their teachings, to silence them in whole or in part, and even to require them to deny their teachings or face the severest penalties. But the scientific findings of Galileo and others were inevitably so much more powerful in their impact upon the minds of the educated that that power of the church was doomed. The authority claimed by both philosophers and theologians and claimed for Scripture in many areas of human experience was destined to be greatly reduced and restricted. That process inescapably raised in a new and critical way the issue of just what Scripture is, how it came to be, how it should be interpreted, and what kind of authority it has, and these questions entailed questions of what revelation is and how God acts. The truth of Christianity that had long been assumed would also come into question. It would be some time after Galileo before all of this would become manifest, but some church leaders were quick to see a very real threat.

Nevertheless, the Roman Catholic Church made no hasty condemnation of Galileo and his teachings, nor, indeed, of Copernicus. Galileo was well received in Rome in the year following the publication of *The Starry Messenger*. Stillman Drake has described that visit as "a triumphal tour," noting that besides being welcomed by church officials and noblemen, Galileo was accorded a pleasant interview with Pope Paul V, and the mathematicians of the faculty of the Roman College confirmed Galileo's findings (ibid., 75).

Of course, there had been relatively little time for the issues to become clear and opposition to develop. This was no longer true in 1615 when Cardinal Bellarmine wrote to the author of a book defending Galileo's teachings,

> it appears to me that Your Reverence and Sig. Galileo did prudently to content yourselves with speaking hypothetically and not positively, as I have always believed Copernicus did. For to say that assuming the earth moves and the sun stands still saves all the appearances better than eccentrics and epicycles is to speak well. This has no danger in it, and it suffices for mathematicians. But to wish to affirm that the sun is really fixed in the center of the heavens and merely turns upon itself without travelling from east to west, and that the earth is situated in the third sphere and revolves very swiftly around the sun, is a very dangerous thing, not only by irritating the theologians and scholastic philosophers, but also by injuring our holy faith and making the sacred Scripture false. (Ibid., 162–63)

The case that Cardinal Bellarmine offered in support of these last two very serious judgments was erroneous. Strictly speaking the church could accommodate Galileo's specific teachings without violation of anything officially a part of the faith or of the accepted principles of scriptural interpretation. Yet the judgments he expressed were quite natural and history has shown him right in the fear that Galileo's work would raise serious questions about the Bible and the Christian faith.

The suggestion that the new science be taught as a hypothesis useful to mathematicians but not asserted to be true sounds today like an encouragement to dishonesty, but in its own time it was far more plausible. Prior to Galileo's work astronomical theories were defended in terms of mathematical harmony and simplicity and were properly to be regarded as hypotheses. It is likely that the cardinal did not recognize that something essentially different was being presented by Galileo, for while he had not proven the Copernican theory, he had offered impressive empirical evidence instead of mathematical beauty, and he had shown basic tenets of the traditional cosmology to be false.

Galileo, in any case, was convinced of the truth of his teachings and not to be satisfied with prudent discussions of hypotheses. He vigorously proclaimed his own conclusions, and the church came to the defense of its own authority. In 1616 Galileo's teachings were censured, he was admonished to abandon the opinions under dispute, and he was evidently enjoined from teaching, defending, or discussing them. And at approximately the same time the Congregation of the Index decreed the Copernican theory to be false and contrary to Scripture, suspended *On the Revolutions of the Heavenly Spheres* "until corrected," and condemned and banned books that defended the Copernican theory as true.

Galileo was able to remain quiet for a while but, provoked by teachings he was convinced were false and encouraged by the election to the papacy of an old friend and defender, Cardinal Barberini—now Urban VIII—he wrote his *Dialogue of the Two Principal Systems of the World,* seeking a definitive establishment of the Copernican theory as against the Ptolemaic. He finished it in 1630 and was able to obtain permission for the publication in 1632. Galileo was summoned to Rome and put on trial primarily for violation of the admonition and injunction of 1616. In 1633 he was found guilty, his book was banned, and he was required (with at least a verbal threat of torture) to repudiate his teachings.

This humiliation of Galileo was in the long run a greater humiliation for the church. Galileo had inaugurated the science that was dramatically to change our lives and our ways of understanding ourselves and our world. The church's defensive reaction began a long period of misguided attempts to cling to authority it did not possess and to identify the doctrinal formulations of one cultural setting with the truth of faith itself. But we do well to remember that the degree of rightness in Galileo and the degree of error in the church were by no means obvious at that time. On the one hand, much had yet to be learned before Galileo's vindication would be clearly established. On the other hand, the change that this development of science set in motion was so vast and so deep that it would be utterly unrealistic to suppose it could have been readily accepted. That we are relatively more prepared to accept certain kinds of change today is largely the result—directly and indirectly —of the development of science.

There is yet another aspect of Galileo's teachings that was to have enormous implications in succeeding generations: his interpretation of the character of nature. All of nature in his view is to be understood as matter in motion, and accordingly what is real in nature is what may be described mathematically. Note here that the earlier practice of moving from philosophy to science has been reversed, Galileo is now deriving philosophical generalizations from his scientific conclusions. As Barbour puts it, "What Galileo did was to extrapolate from his own work; he assumed that the ultimate constituents of nature were exhaustively describable *in the same categories* that he found to be so powerful in analyzing the motion of observable objects" (Barbour 1966, 27).

This is especially clear in Galileo's development of the distinction of primary and secondary qualities. For some this is but a way of distinguishing those characteristics necessary for something to be what it is from those characteristics not necessary to it. For example, one need not have hair on one's head to be a human being, but without some capacity for reason one is not fully human. But Galileo held that the secondary qualities are not truly in the objects in relation to which we experience them, but are due rather to our way of experiencing them through the senses. Galileo was firmly convinced that he had shown how human understanding of the cosmos was basically misunderstood because of naiveté about the way in which it is seen. In this distinction of primary and secondary qualities, he was now arguing that major aspects of all of our experience are misunderstood because we have been naive about the ways in which we perceive. Because of our vantage point the sun appears to move around the earth. Because of our senses things appear to have color, taste, and odor. Galileo believed us misled in both cases. Galileo had, he believed, offered a better knowledge of the cosmos and of motion in general by observation, experimentation, and mathematical interpretation. He inferred that nature *is* as it is known in this way. Here at its beginnings are clear signs of science leading to scientism. Here are initial steps in the development of a mechanistic interpretation of nature and even of the whole of reality.

Galileo's work was hardly sufficient by itself to bring about such a thoroughgoing change of basic perspective. But others were soon to follow up and seek solutions for problems he had uncovered and left unsolved. A particularly glaring gap left in his treatment of the solar system had to do specifically with the motion of planets on which he had done so much. He had effectively undermined the belief that they circle the earth, and he had shown (at least in the cases of the moon and the sun) that these "heavenly bodies" were not characterized by the supposed perfection of a higher element. This last threw considerable doubt on the old belief that those bodies were moved by invisible higher "intelligences." Kepler had still been content to find mathematical perfection in their movements even if they were ellipses rather than circles, but the spirit of inquiry that we have seen developing was not to be satisfied without a better understanding of why these bodies moved as they did. The understanding of inertia was not sufficient, for that would account only for movement in a straight line. In addition the question was left open as to why the planets all moved in almost the same plane.

René Descartes (1596–1650) was one of the first to grapple with these problems and offer a solution that had considerable influence. That solution was shown by Newton to be inconsistent with observation, but it is important for the concerns of the present study to note the general character of that solution and its contrast to medieval ways of interpretation.

Descartes's explanation was in terms of a theory of vortices, and it presupposed that space, rather than being empty, was filled with a fluidlike matter or ether. Hence,

> as a straw floating on water is caught in an eddy and whirled to the center of motion, so a falling stone is drawn to the Earth and a satellite towards its planet, while the Earth and the planet, with their attendant and surrounding vortices, are whirled in a greater vortex round the sun. (Dampier 1966, 136)

What is important about this theory, as Dampier states, is that "it was a bold attempt to reduce the stupendous problem of the sky to dynamics. . . . It reduced the physical Universe to a vast machine, expressible . . . in mathematical terms" (ibid., 136–37). This whole mode of understanding the world

> was fundamentally different from the still prevalent views of Plato and Aristotle and the Schoolmen, according to whom God had created the world in order that, through man the crown of it all, the whole process might return to God. In Descartes' scheme, God endowed the Universe with motion at the beginning, and afterwards allows it to run spontaneously, though in accordance with His will. It is pictured as material rather than spiritual, indifferent rather than teleological. God, ceasing to be the Supreme Good, is relegated to the position of a First Cause. (Ibid., 137)

It is generally agreed that it was Sir Isaac Newton (1642–1727) who worked out the very complex mathematical problems and put together the various relevant findings and suggestions that had been developed in such fashion as to offer what long seemed to be a definitive interpretation of the workings of the universe. It was this achievement that not only earned him the reputation of being one of the greatest men of history, but also established the growing dominance of the mathematical-mechanical understanding of reality for some two centuries.

It is likely that people are more often puzzled than enlightened by the familiar jocular references to Newton's discovering the law of gravity and solving the problems of the motions of the planets by a sudden insight upon observing (or being struck by) an apple falling in an orchard. However true or untrue the stories of the apple may be, the bringing together under the same principles of interpretation of the movements of such small bodies falling at the earth's surface with the movements of the moon and planets was a major achievement. The very puzzling nature of the comparison of two such unlike occurrences is a small measure of the significance of the achievement. A tiny object falling *vertically* for a few feet surely seems to have very little in common with an enormous body like the moon *circling* the earth at a distance of approximately a quarter of a million miles.

Actually the idea of gravity was far from new with Newton. The general idea had been proposed and worked with by many persons. What was lacking was mathematical clarification and demonstration that would change a very unclear general idea into a useful tool of scientific understanding. Newton showed that the continual deflection of the moon away from inertial movement in a straight line and toward the earth was in accordance with the hypothesis that the force producing this "fall" varies inversely as the square of the distance between the two bodies. He tested whether by this assumption he could predict the rate of fall of objects at the earth's surface, and found the observations to be sufficiently close. He was further able to show that the same force proportionate to the product of the masses of the bodies (and inversely proportional to the square of the distances between them) would account for the motions of the planets in relation to the sun in accordance with Kepler's laws. Indeed, he was able to apply this principle successfully to the relations of planets to satellites, to the paths of comets, to the understandings of the tides of the oceans as a result of the attractions among earth, moon, and sun, and in effect to any bodies or bits of matter in the universe.

One of the greater difficulties had been that the calculations had all been based upon the assumption that one could regard the various bodies such as the sun and the planets as though they were points (that is, that all of the attractive force was concentrated in the centers of the various bodies). This hardly seemed justified until Newton carried out the very complex mathematical calculations showing that this was indeed the result of applying the same principle to the relations of the various particles of the various bodies to each other.

One of the more graphic illustrations of the influence and the success of Newton's system came in 1846, almost 160 years after the publication of his *Principia,* when it was recognized that there were irregularities in the orbit of the planet Uranus that could not adequately be accounted for in terms of the other known bodies. It was assumed, therefore, that there must be another planet, previously undiscovered, which would account for these irregularities. J. C. Adams of Cambridge and the French mathematician Leverrier, working separately, were able by calculating from the available data and in terms of Newton's principles to determine just where such a planet should be. When the Berlin telescope was focused according to these calculations, there was the planet! This is the planet now called Neptune.

It is only fair to note here that a few years later irregularities were discovered in the orbit of Mercury, but the same procedures failed to disclose the expected new planet. The factors that led to the breakdown of the supposed finality of the Newtonian system need not concern us here, however.

What is of particular interest here is the vast change the development of science wrought in our common assumptions concerning ourselves and the world in which we live. The foregoing sketches have omitted far more than they have included, but they should provide a sufficient reminder to permit some summary of that change, a change of outlook and understanding that has been growing gradually for the past three centuries.

Before the scientific developments of the seventeenth century the Christian citizens of Europe could take considerable comfort in the conviction that whatever particular difficulties might beset them, they were nevertheless the focus of the creative work of God just as their earth was the center of the whole creation. Even though a few wild speculators had suggested from time to time that the natural and revealed understanding of the universe might be in error, this was simply a matter for the scholars to argue about, and besides the "clear" teachings of the Bible, it was "obvious" that such speculations were not consistent with the centrality of Jesus Christ for the whole of creation, history, and redemption. The purposes of God were the ultimate basis of explanation of things, and the theologians and philosophers were the ones who guided the understanding thereof. The presence and the activity of God were "known" to be everywhere, and unusual events were therefore to be understood in this light. A bright star might herald the birth of a king or messiah, and a comet might portend disaster for the Saxons in 1066. A plague would indicate the anger of God and suggest the wisdom of building a new cathedral or periodically devoting the central labors of a community to the performance of the Passion Drama.

The scientific developments of the seventeenth century shattered such a "world view." The effect was far from immediate and universal, but it was widespread and has grown ever since. In principle neither the reality of God as Creator and Judge, nor that of Jesus Christ as Redeemer, nor the authoritative role of Scripture was denied. But the way in which these things were understood was altered, and questions were inevitably raised where previously things were taken for granted.

Possibly the greatest indication of these changes lies in the recognition of the shift regarding how certain issues are to be settled, as previously noted in connection with Galileo's struggles with the church. In the time of Cusanus it could be argued that the universe must be of indeterminate size and include many worlds because that would be more appropriate to the infinite glory of God. And such an argument could be countered by noting that it would require many Christs and was therefore obviously absurd. In Copernicus's time it could be argued that the sun rather than the earth is at the center of the universe because this offers a simpler harmony of movements, and that could be accepted for purposes of calendar calculations and the convenience of the mathematicians but refuted as to the question of truth on grounds that it was contrary to the teachings of Scripture, Aristotle, and the church fathers. In Galileo's time it could be asserted that telescopes produced illusions, and the Inquisition could determine whether or not one could teach new understandings of the world.

The general influence of this kind of appeal to the authority of the Bible, the church, the theologians, and the philosophers in all matters, including even natural science, did not disappear overnight. Indeed, one can point today to various instances of similar appeals such as that group which has been reported to claim that the whole drama of the moon landings is a gigantic hoax or those persons who refuse the aid of medical science. But the reason why we know of these and similar instances is that they are so peculiar as to be newsworthy, and they are quickly reported to everyone by means of technological achievements, such as radio and television, that have been made possible by the developments of science.

Thus, while the general influence of appeals to theological authority in the areas we now call natural science was not immediately removed, it has been in retreat and on the defensive since the scientific developments of the seventeenth century.

The extent of that retreat has very probably been increased by the tactics of the defense. Yet the ease with which we may today make accusations against earlier defenders of the authority of the church is often a measure of our own failure to recognize the depth of the change we have been seeking herein to glimpse. We think it stupid of the church to have sought to suppress the teachings of Galileo, but we usually do so by naively assuming that what is "obvious" to us today should have been obvious to persons whose most natural way of understanding their world was deeply in conflict with Galileo's teachings. Some people had more common sense than others regarding how to deal with such new perspectives, and the whole matter might have been handled better, but we should not judge seventeenth-century reactions by twentieth-century assumptions.

It would seem that it was inevitable that the authority of church and Scripture would suffer from the fact that in the prescientific era claims of authority were made by the church and for the Bible which in another era would be untenable. The very fact that the claims had been made and then jealously clung to has had the effect of increasing general doubt about any kind of authority for church and Scripture. All the arguments that opposed the new astronomy by appeals to Scripture could only in the long run cast doubt on the veracity of the Bible in the minds of many people who are not patient with later admissions of the theologians that inappropriate claims had been made for scriptural authority.

Logically, the only direct challenge in the matter of biblical authority was to the view that the Bible should be understood to be divinely guaranteed to be without any error when interpreted in a literal sense. This doctrine of plenary verbal inspiration and literalism that was developed by sixteenth-century Protestant Scholasticism could not and cannot be coherently maintained together with natural science, though, needless to say, the tortured efforts to have both together continue to our own time. When these efforts are examined, it is readily seen that literal meanings are not consistently maintained, even where it can be made clear just what is meant by "literal." It should be carefully noted, however, that a doctrine of scriptural inerrancy need not be coupled with literalism, and when the latter is surrendered—or never asserted in the first place as with both traditional Roman Catholic teaching and that of the great Reformers—the direct conflict with natural science is in principle removed. In its place the problem of determining how particular passages should be interpreted is raised, and as we have noticed in connection with the struggles between Galileo and the Inquisition, the traditional pattern of claiming that this is purely and simply the domain of the theologians cannot be consistently maintained, for the progress of scientific discovery has shown that certain passages could not be taken literally—no matter what the theologians might say on the issue.

Indirectly the rise of modern science contributed significantly to the critical raising of an even more basic question concerning the interpretation of Scripture. In radically changing the understanding of the universe from the spirit-filled and theologically defined world of the Middle Ages to the mathematical-mechanical world of "natural law," the rise of science opened in a very critical way the whole question of how God acts. The movement of scientific discoveries kept filling the gaps for which appeal was made to the activity of God until Laplace could (according to the story) answer Napoleon's question of where there was a place for God in his theory with his famous "Sire, I have no need of that hypothesis." As the heavens, the thunderstorms, and the plagues have been more and more understood by science, the credibility of notions of a causally intervening God has been more and more reduced, and it has become increasingly important for the theologians to seek to clarify what is meant by statements about the activity of God. This development was one of the factors preparing the way for the critical examination of the *assumption* that the Bible is in some simple sense a work of God. It opened the way for the consideration of the possibility that the Bible should be understood as being directly a work of humans. It is on this possibility that modern biblical scholarship is founded, and this issue is one of the crucial lines of division between modern and premodern theologies.

Another very important area of both direct and indirect influence of the development of science upon theology that we have touched upon is that of the relationship of philosophy and theology. The direct influence was at the point of the empirical undermining of certain teachings of Aristotle that had become parts of both Roman Catholic and Protestant orthodoxies. This has provided ready ammunition for those who have enjoyed attacking Aristotelian theologies, and it has been easy to say that these particular conflicts with science were a quite unnecessary result of the error of using philosophy for the interpretation of Christian faith rather than holding strictly to "the biblical perspective." When these issues are put in this oversimplified way—as they often have been—they show an interesting failure to grasp the more basic lesson that this encounter with science would gradually make clearer and clearer. This is the lesson that the efforts of the theologians to interpret the Christian faith not only should not be irrevocably tied to any one particular philosophical system, but should not be tied to *any* one specific way of formulating an understanding, because all such formulations, including the scientific, will deeply reflect peculiarities of the particular cultural setting within which or for which they are developed. Science had directly contradicted some points of Aristotle's teaching. More important, it had challenged and changed the very ways in which Western persons understood their world and themselves. In doing so it changed the effective meaning of *all* earlier ways of interpreting and understanding.

WORKS CITED

Aquinas, T., Saint
1945   *Basic Writings of Saint Thomas Aquinas.* 2 vols. Edited and Annotated with an Introduction by Anton C. Pegis. New York: Random House.

Aristotle
1941   *The Basic Works of Aristotle.* Edited and with an Introduction by Richard McKeon. New York: Random House.

Barbour, I. G.
1966   *Issues in Science and Religion.* Englewood Cliffs, N.J.: Prentice-Hall.

Brodrick, J., S.J.
1964   *Galileo: The Man, His Work, His Misfortunes.* New York: Harper & Row.

Burtt, E. A.
1932   *The Metaphysical Foundations of Modern Physical Science.* Rev. ed. London: Routledge & Kegan Paul.

Butterfield, H.
1957   *The Origins of Modern Science: 1300–1800.* New York: Macmillan Co.

Copernicus, N.
1939   *On the Revolutions of the Heavenly Spheres.* Translated by C. G. Wallis. In Great Books of the Western World, editor-in-chief Robert Maynard Hutchins, vol. 16. Chicago: Encyclopaedia Britannica.

Cusanus, N.
1954   *Of Learned Ignorance.* Translated by Fr. Germain Heron. Introduction by D. J. B. Hawkins. New Haven: Yale University Press.

Dampier, W. C.
1966   *A History of Science: And Its Relations with Philosophy and Religion.* 4th ed. Cambridge: Cambridge University Press.

Galileo
1957   *Discoveries and Opinions of Galileo.* Translated with an Introduction and Notes by Stillman Drake. Garden City, N.Y.: Doubleday Anchor Books.

Kepler, J.
1939   *Epitome of Copernican Astronomy.* Translated by C. G. Wallis. In Great Books of the Western World, editor-in-chief Robert Maynard Hutchins, vol. 16. Chicago: Encyclopaedia Britannica.

Koyré, A.
1957   *From the Closed World to the Infinite Universe.* Baltimore: Johns Hopkins Press.

Kuhn, T. S.
    1959   *The Copernican Revolution: Planetary Astronomy in the Develop-
                    ment of Western Thought.* New York: Vintage Books, Random
                    House.

Langford, J. J.
    1966   *Galileo, Science and the Church.* Foreword by Stillman Drake.
                    New York: Desclee Co.

Ptolemy
    1948   *The Almagest.* Translated by R. C. Taliaferro. In Great Books
                    of the Western World, editor-in-chief Robert Maynard Hutch-
                    ins, vol. 16. Chicago: Encyclopaedia Britannica.

2
UNDERSTANDING
THE NEW
WORLD

*The Beginnings
of Modern
Philosophy*

IT WAS INEVITABLE that changes in outlook as deep as those required by the seventeenth-century scientific revolution would have profound effects upon philosophy and through philosophy upon theology. Modern philosophy is, in fact, dated from the seventeenth century and René Descartes (1596–1650) is usually named its founder, because, as Bertrand Russell put it, "He is the first man of high philosophic capacity whose outlook is profoundly affected by the new physics and astronomy" (Russell 1945, 557).

The authority of Aristotle had been attacked by the Renaissance, and the authority of the Church of Rome had been seriously undermined by the Reformation. The scientific revolution seemed effectively to refute the authority of Aristotle, church, and the Bible, and together with these would-be sources of knowledge and security it removed many of the common assumptions in terms of which people had experienced their world.

It was in this situation that Descartes articulated a new method for obtaining knowledge and with it a new understanding of the world. He was a mathematician and physicist as well as a philosopher, and he inaugurated a philosophic revolution because he applied the methods of mathematics not only to the specific problems of science but also to the full breadth of philosophic problems.

In his *Discourse on Method*, Descartes described in a sort of intellectual autobiography how he early recognized that his studies offered him only doubts and errors instead of knowledge. As compared with other fields of study, he said,

> I was especially pleased with mathematics, because of the certainty and self-evidence of its proofs; but I did not yet see its true usefulness, and thinking that it was good only for the mechanical arts, I was astonished that nothing more noble had been built on so firm and solid a foundation. (Descartes 1950, 5)

Borrowing from—yet criticizing—the procedures of logic, analytic geometry, and algebra, Descartes developed a fourfold method for obtaining genuine knowledge of everything that the human mind is capable of understanding. First, never accept anything as true that does not present itself so clearly and distinctly to the mind as to be beyond doubt. Second, divide all problems into as many parts as needed to make simple solutions possible. Third, proceed in an orderly fashion beginning with that which is easiest to understand and moving gradually toward the more complex. Fourth, review the whole procedure carefully and repeatedly to be sure that nothing has been omitted (ibid., 12–13).

In order to find something that was so clear and distinct as to be beyond doubt, Descartes attacked the problem precisely at the point of doubt. His procedure was to reject as false anything that was in any way subject to doubt in order to see whether there was anything that could not be doubted. Since we know that our senses sometimes mislead us, sense data are always subject to doubt. Even the geometers sometimes make mistakes in their reasoning, so reason is not wholly to be trusted. One can also doubt whatever enters one's mind, for the same ideas come to us when asleep as when awake. These very efforts to cast doubt upon everything, however, established beyond any doubt that this doubter, this thinker, must necessarily exist. Here was a conclusion that could not be doubted, for the very effort to doubt it demonstrated its truth. By this "methodological doubt," Descartes made "I think, therefore I am" the first principle of his philosophy (ibid., 21).

This certainty of one's own existence may seem to be neither a very clear and distinct idea nor a fruitful basis for further conclusions, but Descartes believed himself able to establish both the nature of the self and a great many other basic certainties from this starting point. In the first place, the doubting established not only *that* he existed, but that he existed *as a thinking thing*, and in Descartes's judgment this established the entire essence of the self, that it is a thinking thing. This in turn provided the basis of a fundamental distinction in his philosophy, the distinction of mind from body.

> On the ground that, if I had ceased to think while all the rest of what I imagined remained true, I would have had no reason to believe that I had existed, I concluded that I was a substance whose soul essence or nature was only to think, and which, to exist, has no need of space nor of any material thing. Thus it follows that this ego, this soul, by which I am what I am, is entirely distinct from the body and is easier to know than the latter, and that even if the body were not, the soul would not cease to be all that it is. (Ibid.)

Mind and body, then, are two fundamentally different things. While thinking (understood broadly to include all activities of the mind) is the essence of mind, extension (taking up space) is the whole essence of body. In the early stages of the argument, however, while this distinction is basic, the whole question of whether any bodies exist remains open.

Descartes's way of resolving that question was by moving from the certainty of the self's existence to the establishment of the existence of God. He argued that his act of doubting showed imperfection in himself, it being clear to him that knowing is more perfect than doubting. He then asked what source could have provided him with the idea of something more perfect than himself. It could not come from nothing, and he judged it equally unreasonable to suppose that the more perfect could come from the less perfect. "Thus the only hypothesis left was that this idea was put in my mind by a nature that was really more perfect than I was, which had all the perfections that I could imagine, and which was, in a word, God" (ibid., 22). By this process Descartes was not attempting to deduce the existence of God so much as to show that the idea of God is *innate,* and that if we will pause to examine it carefully, we will recognize that God must exist. A perfect being is one characterized by necessary existence, which is to say, it is a being that cannot not be, for were it capable of ceasing to be or of not being, it would hardly be perfect. It follows—he argued—that anyone who understands the meaning of the word "God" knows that God is. It is true necessarily, by definition. God could no more be nonexistent than could a triangle have more or less than three sides (ibid., 23–24).

Descartes insisted that this innate idea of God was quite clear and distinct, more so indeed than any other idea (Descartes 1967, 166). He did not mean by this that he thoroughly comprehended the reality of God. The clarity had to do with the presence of the idea in one's mind. The distinctness was a matter of that kind of knowledge which prevented the possibility of confusion with anything else. When one understood the idea of God and recognized that there could be only one infinite and perfect being, there was no danger of confusion. The idea was then thoroughly clear and distinct and therefore not to be doubted (ibid., 241).

Further, even though Descartes's procedure led first to the certainty of one's own existence as a thinking thing and then to the assurance of the existence of God, once this route had been traversed, it became evident that the idea of God is prior to that of the self, since, Descartes argued, without the idea of a being more perfect than myself, I could not know doubt or desire or anything lacking to me (ibid., 166). And this knowledge of God is not only the precondition of knowledge of the self, but of any and all knowledge. Since that Being from which we have our existence as thinking beings cannot be a deceiver—for truthfulness is a characteristic of perfection—we may be assured that when we reason carefully and perceive clearly and distinctly we are not being deceived (ibid., 172).

Given this assurance, Descartes was confident that he could deduce a great many other truths. As he put it in the *Discourse,*

> I have not only succeeded in satisfying myself in this short time on all the princi-
> pal difficulties usually treated in philosophy, but have also discovered certain
> laws which God has so established in nature, and the notion of which he has so
> fixed in our minds, that after sufficient reflection we cannot doubt that they are
> exactly observed in all which exists or which happens in the world. (Descartes
> 1950, 27)

And in *The Principles of Philosophy* he affirmed "that there is no phenomenon of nature whose explanation has been omitted in this treatise" (Descartes 1901, 354). For the certainty of the existence of God provided the basis not only for trusting the reasonings of the geometers, but also for a degree of confidence in what we may learn through the senses. In this latter instance, however, it is not of such things as "light, color, sounds, odors, tastes, heat, cold, and other tactile qualities" that we may have knowledge, but only of the arithmetic and geometric characteristics (Descartes 1967, 164, 180, 191).

The universe that Descartes described was not, however, as much mathematical as mechanical, at least in his later writings. In his mechanical universe Descartes sought to account for all effects in terms of the impact of bodies upon bodies. There were no natural motions such as bodies falling toward the center, nor any effects of "intelligences" such as had moved the planets according to earlier theories. Nor did God "interfere." God had established the laws of this mechanical world and maintained them as well as the constancy of the total amount of motion, but no special appeals to divine intervention were appropriate (Descartes 1950, 29).

The pervasiveness of Descartes's mechanical interpretation of the material world is illustrated by his depiction of the human body as a machine. This is evident in his description and explanation of the functioning of the heart and circulation of the blood in the *Discourse on Method,* and more broadly applied in his description of the body in his *On the Formation of the Foetus.* The idea of the human body as a machine was hardly new, but as Emile Bréhier points out,

> the idea that the body is a machine is linked traditionally to another idea—to the
> idea that the body is an instrument for the soul that uses it as a mechanic would
> do. We find nothing like this in Descartes, whose machine is constructed and
> made to function in accordance with the universal laws of nature, with the result
> that there is no need . . . for a particular mechanic. (Bréhier 1966, 94)

This is not to suggest that the mind had no role to play, but Descartes's philosophy had difficulties here because of his basic distinction of mind and body. Taken strictly, this should mean that the two could not interact at all for there would be no commonality in terms of which they might make "contact." Apart from appeal to God as the provider of this contact, however, Descartes did offer a theory according to which this interaction takes place through the pineal gland. "Descartes inferred from its structure and location that it could be shaken by the slightest disturbance in the flow of animal spirits moving upward from the heart or sense organs into the 'cavities' of the brain or descending from the brain into the muscles" (ibid., 104). The mind also affects the body through this same organ. In accordance with the laws of the operation of a machine, however, it cannot change the quantity of motion in the body, but it can change the direction of that motion, influencing the flow of spirits to the brain or the muscles.

If one asks how, on this mechanical basis, Descartes would account for human emotions or passions, the reply would further illustrate this mechanical orientation. The emotions, which are related specifically to the soul, are, nevertheless, "engendered, continued and augmented by a particular motion of the animal spirits" (ibid., 102). Such motions are therefore a part of the study of the mechanics of the body, and Descartes believed it possible to discover the particular motions relating to each emotion.

While developing this mathematical-mechanical understanding of human being and of the universe and proposing a new method for gaining knowledge modeled upon the mathematical sciences, Descartes was breaking with tradition in some decisive ways, but he had no desire to be other than a loyal son of the Roman Catholic Church. He took pains to insist that his teachings were in no way intended to conflict with those founded on revelation. The latter are, he held, to be believed whether we can comprehend them or not (Descartes 1901, 310) and are "incomparably more certain than anything else" (ibid., 333). He added at the end of his *Principles of Philosophy* that he submitted all of his opinions to the authority of the church (ibid., 361).

It might at first be supposed today that Descartes had little to fear in this regard. He not only devoted considerable attention to affirming the existence of God, but he made all knowledge dependent upon the trustworthiness of God. But while such affirmations from a scientist-philosopher might sound supportive of faith today, the very questions Descartes raised and the way in which he raised them as well as the answers he gave had enormous implications for the traditional understandings of Christianity.

In tackling the problem of *method* for obtaining knowledge Descartes was effectively focusing attention upon his recognition that the new science had seriously called the traditional authorities into question. For centuries the dominant pattern had been one in which the ground rules and the boundary lines had been set by theology. Philosophy had had to operate within those limitations, and science had had to follow the lead of both theology and philosophy. Now this situation was reversed, and the findings of science were setting the problems for philosophy which in turn was beginning to define new rules for theology.

Further, the proposed new method, following the example of mathematical science, not only illustrated the change to a new kind of authority, but also led to the mathematical-mechanical description of the world, a major step in the process of "edging" God out of our everyday world, almost reducing the deity to the role of first cause. Although Descartes had to appeal to God to fill certain gaps in his explanations, that very practice reduced God's role and foreshadowed a continuing reduction as science (and philosophy building upon science) gradually removed these gaps.

Despite his protestations to the contrary, Descartes was thoroughly undercutting the traditional appeals to revelation, because he was approaching and solving his problems without any appeal to revelation. One might say he left revelation standing by the roadside. Reason became here the principal instrument of knowledge, including knowledge of God.

It was inevitable that in Descartes's focusing of the attention of philosophy on the general problem of knowledge, the more specific problem of religious knowledge would be entailed. On what basis can persons claim to have knowledge of the nature and the will of God? Much of the traditional assumption had built upon remarkable occurrences that were interpreted as direct causal intervention by God. Modern science had begun the process of explaining such events on very different grounds, and on such grounds the philosophers were developing an interpretation of the world that had little if any place for such interventions. In addition, the impact of these events was through the data of the senses (the hearing of a voice, the seeing of a burning bush, a strange star, or an inexplicable cure). Philosophers such as Descartes were now raising serious questions about the nature and reliability of sense data. If, however, one turns to a doctrine of "inner illuminations" whereby God's revelation is held to reach persons without use of the senses, this is making an appeal to grounds quite beyond verification in a time when verification is more and more being demanded, and it is turning away from what can be seen and measured precisely when the success of the sciences is being built upon the empirical foundation.

For the most part the churches simply insisted upon their doctrines and their authority, but the success of the scientific spirit doomed this tactic. Others, as we shall note, sought to reinterpret Christian faith in terms of the new understandings of the world, but, as we shall also note (especially in the work of David Hume), they were not able to escape the difficulties of the epistemological problem. Eventually the theologians found it necessary to seek new understandings of revelation, a process given particular impetus by the work of Immanuel Kant, that continues today.

Descartes not only made this problem of knowledge central in his work, he also may be said to have complicated that problem by his sharp distinction of mind and body. That distinction was already implicit in the concentration of science upon the material world, for the human minds that were developing the scientific understandings were not accessible to the methods of study employed. It was Descartes, however, who made this problem not only explicit but extreme. His setting apart of the mind from the material world necessarily made acute the question of how we might have knowledge of that world. Descartes has been much criticized for this "bifurcation," as if the distinction and its problems need not have arisen, but the struggles of succeeding philosophers—to the present—to solve those problems indicate their genuineness.

Descartes's own approach to these problems is what is called "rationalistic," which in the context of the problem of knowledge means that his major emphasis in seeking knowledge was upon the role of reason rather than upon sense experience. Those who place greatest weight upon the latter are called "empiricists." This is not to suggest that Descartes had no use for observation and experimentation. He insisted upon them. His basic emphasis, however, was upon the role of reason, which, as we noted, had to establish the very possibility of empirical knowledge.

In this emphasis Descartes was building upon the mathematical side of the new science, and the resulting rationalism remained dominant among continental philosophers for a substantial period. The empirical emphasis of the new science, the dependence upon observation, experiment, and, in general, sense data, became dominant among other philosophers, particularly in Britain. We shall note this development briefly in the philosophies of John Locke, George Berkeley, and David Hume.

THE EMPIRICISTS

Generally speaking, people are what the philosophers call "naive realists" in epistemology. We are not even aware that there is a problem of knowledge in the philosophers' sense. I simply assume that the paper and pen, the desk and the chair, the room and its furniture and all of the other things in my present experience of writing are in themselves exactly as I see them. They are there for others and even for angels and demons—if there should be any—just precisely as they are here for me. In this view there is no problem of knowledge. The real is what I see and hear and taste and touch and smell, and I know their reality precisely as it is conveyed to me by my senses. Probably the most important reason so few people in our culture believe in angels and demons is that our senses do not convey anything concerning such beings to us.

However, brief reflection on the matter soon reveals at least two considerations that show so simple an appeal to sense data to be insufficient. In the first place, there are important issues that are not basically questions of sense experience. Suppose one asks whether a particular tax is *just* or whether a particular action is *right*. Most of us have very firm convictions about what is just or unjust and what is right or wrong. How do we know? Do we know?

Second, we have all found from time to time that we have been mistaken about what we thought we saw or heard or felt. Descartes emphasized this point in his arguments that sense data are subject to doubt and not therefore a reliable foundation for knowledge. Nor was this simply the strange academic interest of a philosopher. The struggles between Copernicus, Galileo, and other scientists and the authorities had much to do with the problem of interpreting sense data. It certainly looks as though the sun moves around the earth, and it hardly feels as though the earth is hurtling around the sun or spinning on its own axis. The development of science neither was then nor is now supportive of naive realism.

John Locke (1632–1704) taught that all our knowledge comes to us from experience, but he was no naive realist. On the contrary, he subjected the processes of human experience to very extensive analysis. This was no doubt partly the result of the impact of the new science upon him. He was trained in the field of medicine and he belonged to the Royal Society. However, the impetus for his famous *Essay Concerning Human Understanding* (1690) was not simply the academic question whether the methods so successful in the sciences could be fruitfully employed in such areas as ethics and religion. He was deeply involved in the political struggles of his time, specifically against the Anglican theocracy. He was especially concerned with criticizing two doctrines, the so-called divine right of kings with its claim to absolute power, and the further claim that the power of the monarch included the spiritual realm and therefore the right to impose doctrine and forms of worship upon the people. In Locke's judgment such doctrines were based not upon knowledge but prejudice. How might this be established? His procedure was to examine critically the very bases and nature of human knowledge.

Descartes had begun this search by doubting whatever he could doubt, including sense data, and had therefore emphasized the role of reason. He argued that apart from God-given innate ideas knowledge would not be possible. His confidence in reason and desire for "clear and distinct" ideas reveal the impact of the mathematical sciences. By contrast, Locke, more impressed by the scientific successes based upon observation and experimentation, argued that *all* contents of human consciousness came from either "sensation" (sense perceptions) or "reflection" upon our own mental states and activities. The latter was not, however, intended to suggest any "innate ideas." Locke was emphatic in his rejection of any such notion. Rather, reflection was a term acknowledging the difference between experiences coming from without and those coming from within. Human experience and knowledge, he sought to show, could be entirely accounted for without any appeal to innate principles or primary notions stamped upon human minds (Locke 1952, 103–4). Our complex ideas result from the mind's combining, comparing, and abstracting of the simple "ideas" (a term indicating any content of consciousness).

One of the more important results of Locke's careful examination of the complex processes that he believed to be required to account for our actual experience was his judgment that a rather large portion of our simple sense impressions does not give us an accurate perception of the object perceived. What one should note here is that in this account of human knowledge, which begins with the affirmation that all of our knowledge comes from experience and most of that from sensation, the reliability of sense data is, in part at least, cast in doubt.

Locke also concluded that our idea of "substances"—realities underlying the characteristics of which we have sense impressions—is but a *supposition* of something that remains unknown to us.

The surprising result of Locke's empiricism in which all human knowledge is explained as dependent upon sensation and reflection is that one is more certain of one's own existence and of God's than of the objects of sense perceptions, a conclusion surprisingly similar to the teachings of Descartes. The demonstrative certainty of God's existence is founded upon the intuitive certainty of one's own existence. We know that we had a beginning and therefore that we were produced by something else. Something does not come from nothing. Therefore there must have been something from all eternity, and that would mean something that did not have a beginning. Further, that eternal something would have to have the power to bestow all other power. Also, since humans have knowledge, that being which is the source of all other being must be a knowing being. Such an eternal, all-powerful, and all-knowing being is, of course, God, and Locke judged that on this basis "we more certainly know that there is a God, than that there is anything else without us" (ibid., 350).

Locke did not restrict knowledge of God to what could in this fashion be demonstrated by reason, for he also affirmed the certainty of doctrines given us by God's revelation. Faith leaves no room for doubt for we cannot doubt the testimony of God (ibid., 371). Locke was aware, however, that that does not settle the question of just when that which is claimed to be God's revelation is God's revelation. Here reason must be the judge. Locke argued, in particular, that no revelation could be contrary to reason (ibid., 387). On this issue Locke stands between the more traditional acceptance of the authority of church and Scripture and the growing desire to replace those by reason. The latter is associated particularly with the "Deists," a very mixed group who generally sought to show the reasonableness of Christianity as over against any attempt to found it upon revelation. Though Locke affirmed revelation, his book on the *Reasonableness of Christianity* (1695) and his insistence upon the role of reason in judging alleged revelations showed the same spirit that was more radically pursued by the Deists. The relationship of the further development of empiricism to the growth of the idea of "natural religion" is something we shall examine in connection with the work of David Hume.

Before turning to Hume, however, we should note the work of George Berkeley (1685–1753), who took his starting point in Locke's conclusions and then sought to follow empiricism even more consistently than Locke had. In particular, Berkeley rejected Locke's teaching on abstract ideas and his distinction of primary and secondary qualities, protesting against the turning of our experienced world filled with colors and sounds into geometrical abstractions. In this point Berkeley is closer to the common view of experience. His conclusion, however, was that *all* perceptions are relative to the perceiver, and that the supposed qualities of things only *are* in being perceived (Berkeley 1957, 24). This is the point of his famous "esse est percipi" —"to be is to be perceived." There is, for example, no desk if there is no perceiver. That is because if we note carefully what the word "desk" means, it turns out that it refers to a collection of perceptions such as brownness, hardness, smoothness, squareness, and so forth. If there is no perceiver present, clearly there will be no such perceptions. What will be "there"? We do not know. We could say that the circumstances remain such that if there were perceivers present, they would have those perceptions we call a "desk."

The oddness of that conclusion is emphasized by Berkeley's critique of Locke's doctrine of substance. Locke had argued that we have no perceptions of substances, but that since we cannot conceive of qualities as existing in and by themselves, we must presume the existence of this unknown and unknowable substratum. In Berkeley's view this inference is entirely unwarranted. It violates Locke's insistence that all knowledge comes from experience. There are no substances underlying qualities (ibid., 26–35).

Given his insistence that all perceptions are relative, dependent upon the perceiver, and his denial of the existence of substances, it is easy to see how Berkeley was taken to be a thoroughgoing subjectivist or as teaching that there is no external world known to us and that we produce our own experience. But this was clearly not Berkeley's intention. First, he held that the ideas (perceptions) come to us quite apart from our willing them or not—indeed, often in spite of what we will. Second, these perceptions convey a very remarkable order. There is a structure and consistency in our experience that is given (ibid., 36–37).

How then does Berkeley interpret and account for this ordered, given experience? Stated far too simply, his answer was that it is the activity of God that confronts us. There is an environment we encounter in our perceptions because God maintains those conditions that make those perceptions possible. Thus the only realities that truly exist are minds, that of God and those of persons, and the ideas in these minds (ibid., 35–104).

Dr. Samuel Johnson is said to have offered a refutation of Berkeley's teaching simply by kicking a stone. This has had great appeal to persons who regard themselves as being guided by practical "common sense." Actually all that Johnson demonstrated was that he did not understand Berkeley, for the latter had never denied that in those circumstances one would have those perceptions of stone, hardness, and so forth. What he had done was to offer a different explanation as to what makes those perceptions possible. It is assuredly a most difficult explanation for "common sense" either to grasp or accept, but it is also worth noting that it is not open to any simple refutation, and it has the philosophical advantage of readily solving the problems entailed in Descartes's division of creation into the two utterly distinct substances of mind and body.

A thoroughgoing empiricism had not yet been achieved, however, at least not in the judgment of David Hume (1711–76). Berkeley had shown that a strict empiricism ruled out belief in substances, but he turned to another metaphysical affirmation to take their place as accounting for the origin of our perceptions, using the whole as an argument for the existence of God. Hume sought to show that if one accepts the empirical principle that all of our ideas come from experience, or, as he put it, that "when we analyze our thoughts or ideas, however compounded or sublime, we always find that they resolve themselves into such simple ideas as were copied from a precedent feeling or sentiment" (Hume 1955, 28), then all such inferences are quite unwarranted. "All such inferences" included all of the arguments whereby the proponents of the then-popular natural religion believed that they could establish the existence and nature of God.

Probably the most striking element in Hume's argument is the conclusion he reached about cause and effect. Given the empiricist conviction that all our ideas originate in simple impressions, how does one justify belief in causal relations? Where does this idea come from? This is no trivial question. Not only did metaphysical and natural theological conclusions presuppose an unexamined concept of cause and effect, also entailed were convictions about morality, politics, rights, obligations, and justice. Indeed, it is an assumption that underlies all aspects of our lives, and Hume recognized that it had vital practical implications as well as far-reaching theoretical ones. He began with an examination of the association of ideas. Just how do the simple impressions become organized in our consciousness? Hume's judgment was that the various ways that might be suggested can be reduced to "only three principles of connection among ideas, namely *Resemblance, Contiguity* in time or place, and *cause* or *effect*" (ibid., 32). The most important of these is the third, for "all reasonings concerning matter of fact seem to be founded on the relation of *cause* and *effect*. By means of that relation alone can we go beyond the evidence of our memory and senses" (ibid., 41). He gave the example of a man finding a watch on a desert island and concluding that other men had been there. He then noted that here and in all reasonings concerning fact there is a supposition "that there is a connection between the present fact and that which is inferred from it" (ibid.).

Where does this idea of a *necessary connection* come from? Hume was well aware that this is not a question at all for most people. We are firmly under the impression that we experience causal relations all the time. Hume was sure that we are mistaken in this; he illustrated his contention by reference to one billiard ball striking another. He argued that we do not in fact see (or otherwise experience) the first ball causing the second one to move. Hume's claim was that it is only the repeated experience of the particular sequence that leads one to expect that the sequence which has been seen consistently before will continue to occur in the same way (ibid., 43). An infant, having been burnt by fire, avoids it. This is not because of any reasoning or any inborn knowledge, nor, said Hume, is it because the child has seen any necessary connection between the fire and the burning sensation. In the case of both the motions of the billiard balls and the fire and the burning, what is observed or experienced is "contiguity," the things coming into contact, and succession, the one factor preceding the other in time. But where does one have an impression of *necessary connection?*

Since we do not receive any sense perceptions of this necessary connection, is it possible that the idea is produced by our reasoning? Hume's answer, of course, was no, but he did take time to examine this issue. He noted, for example, that no one ever supposed that the explosion of gunpowder or the attraction of a lodestone could have been discovered by reasoning that has no recourse to experience. As far as unaided reason can tell us, quite different "effects" from those we have become accustomed to observing are conceivable. "The mind can never possibly find the effect in the supposed cause by the most accurate scrutiny and examination. For the effect is totally different from the cause, and consequently can never be discovered in it" (ibid.).

Having ruled out the possibilities that the idea of necessary connection could have come from either sense impressions or reason, Hume considered the suggestion that it might be derived from our experience of the workings of our own minds, that is, that it might arise from an "internal impression" (ibid., 76). For example, one may decide to raise an arm and then do so, or to call up some image in the mind, thus doing so. In this we judge that we are experiencing a power to bring about certain effects, and we believe that we experience ourselves as causing certain effects. But even here, said Hume, we do not have an impression of necessary connection. In defense of this assertion he argued first that we have no knowledge of the union of soul and body wherein to understand the relation of the wish in the mind to the movement in the body, no more, he said, than we comprehend how to control the movements of the planets by the exercise of our wills (ibid., 76–77). In addition, he argued, we do not have an equal capacity to control the movements of all of the organs of the body. We will the movements of our tongues and fingers, for example, but we do not will the activities of such organs as the heart and the liver. Why this is so he judged unanswerable, for we are not truly conscious of a power to effect the movements in either case (ibid., 77).

Thus the case for the origin of the idea of necessary connection in "internal impressions" is no different from the situation regarding external impressions. We experience the sequence, but how the willing relates to the motion or the image remains utterly unknown (ibid., 78).

Since no origin can be found for the idea of the power or necessary connection presumed operative in relations of cause and effect, Hume concluded that that idea is really without meaning (ibid., 85). Instead of an idea of cause and effect, the mind has what might be called "customary expectations." Because one event is regularly accompanied by another, the mind forms an idea that there is a necessary connection that becomes a strong habitual feeling, but there is no genuine basis for this conviction. When it is said "that one object is connected with another, we mean only that they have acquired a connection in our thought and give rise to this inference by which they become proofs of each other's existence" (ibid., 86). Because we have always experienced certain things such as fire and heat or snow and cold together, the mind develops a habit of belief that where the one is found the other will also be found (ibid., 60). He did not wish to suggest that we ought, therefore, to give up this belief and the attendant expectations. He was quite well aware that not only science but everyday practical life was dependent upon this belief, and that all of this is "a species of natural instincts, which no reasoning or process of the thought and understanding is able either to produce or to prevent" (ibid.). He readily foresaw the obvious objection that his own conduct was based upon the common supposition upon which he was casting doubt.

> My practice, you say, refutes my doubts. But you mistake the purport of my question. As an agent, I am quite satisfied in the point; but as a philosopher who has some share of curiosity, I will not say skepticism, I want to learn the foundation of this inference. (Ibid., 52)

But this was no idle curiosity. The questions involved were not simply those such as whether we should believe in the regularity of nature based upon supposed necessary connections when we are confronted with the possibility of stepping off a high place or of drinking something that has hitherto been observed to be followed by violent reactions. These things are subject to continual verification. But there are other kinds of questions involved. We are always being confronted with assertions in the realms of morality, politics, metaphysics, and theology that often claim to be matters of certain knowledge and that affect our rights and opportunities, our sense of the meaning and purpose of life, the choices we make and the punishments to which we may be subject both here and hereafter. Wars have been fought and tortures inflicted in the name of God. These issues were of great concern to Hume, who by this careful examination of the questions concerning human knowledge was raising basic questions about the claims upon which much human strife was based.

As we have noted earlier, the growing success of the sciences was accompanied by an increasing confidence in the human capacity to explain the nature of reality. Appeals to the traditional authorities carried less and less weight. One can easily see that Hume's work was no comfort to supporters of those traditional authorities. This kind of critical questioning could only be embarrassing to them. He paid what appears to be "lip service" to the view that

Christianity is based upon "faith" and "revelation," but the impact of his work was clearly to cast doubt on claims that particular events or voices or documents are revelations from God (ibid., sec. X).

Hume also launched a powerful attack upon the increasingly popular "natural religion." This "movement" was itself an expression of the growing confidence in the human capacity to explain all things. The empirical methods of the sciences were revealing an ever more remarkable design, harmony, and purposiveness in the whole of nature—or so it was argued. For such a great design, there must surely be a great designer. By such arguments many believed they could establish both the existence and nature of God. Hume subjected such arguments to a powerful critique in his *Dialogues Concerning Natural Religion,* showing that when applied strictly the empiricism upon which those reasonings were allegedly built led to no such conclusions. Without attempting to summarize those discussions here, we may note how the argument from design depends upon the assumption of the necessary connections of cause and effect that Hume had already shown to be subject to doubt from a strict empirical standpoint. In the later dialogues he presented many additional arguments, but in this point alone he had done enough to leave all of the conventional "arguments" for the existence of God in doubt.

The concern here is not with the question of how much trust one can put in arguments for the existence of God. It is rather with seeing the development of the problem of knowledge that has been central to the history of modern philosophy. The success of modern science had both undercut the traditional assumptions and authorities—thus bringing the problem of knowledge into focus—and given rise to possible solutions in the rationalistic approaches following the mathematical emphases of science and the empirical approaches modeled upon the scientific confidence in observation and experiment. The influence of the latter has continued to grow to our own time, so much so that some judge the average citizen of a technologically advanced nation inevitably to be an empiricist—even though that is usually unrecognized. But, to whatever extent that may be true, modern popular empiricism is still naive realism when compared to the conclusions reached by the studies of Locke, Berkeley, and Hume concerning what we know on the basis of a strict examination of human sensation and reflection.

IMMANUEL KANT

The influence of these philosophers was and is great, but the greatest direct impact of the studies of the problem of knowledge did not come from their work. It came rather from the work of Immanuel Kant (1724–1804), who, as he put it, was awakened from his dogmatic slumber by the work of Hume (Kant 1953, 7). This "dogmatic slumber" was the unexamined rationalist assumption that the laws required for coherent reasoning were characteristics of reality itself. Hume did not persuade Kant that we should give up our confidence in the applicability of the principle of causality to the world. In the first place, Kant did not accept the empiricist starting point that all of our ideas are derived from simple impressions, which was fundamental to Hume's argument. Second, Kant was quite convinced of the truth of the Newtonian description of the world, so that if philosophy, as in Hume's case, came to conclusions that could not account for that scientific knowledge, this was not to the detriment of science but of philosophy. (Hume's reduction of physics from knowledge to probability is a much more acceptable position today than it was in his time, and it was quite unacceptable to Kant.) In fact, Kant was convinced that Hume had been misunderstood by his critics.

> The question was not whether the concept of cause was right, useful, and even indispensable for our knowledge of nature, for this Hume had never doubted; but whether that concept could be thought by Reason *a priori,* and consequently whether it possessed an inner truth, independent of all experience, implying a wider application than merely to the objects of experience. This was Hume's problem. It was a question concerning the *origin,* not concerning the *indispensable need* of the concept. (Ibid., 5)

The accuracy of Kant's interpretation of Hume's intention need not concern us here. What Hume's work had revealed to Kant was that rationalism had been proceeding upon unexamined assumptions. By what right could it be assumed that a law of reason such as that of cause and effect was applicable to the world known in experience, thus making scientific knowledge possible?

One way of posing the problem was to ask how we could have a priori knowledge, meaning knowledge not derived from experience. Kant agreed with Hume's argument that we cannot derive from experience the knowledge that every change must have a cause. But, contrary to Hume, Kant was convinced that this was knowledge, thus that we have a priori knowledge. How could this be explained? In order to answer this question Kant developed a new understanding of human knowledge. He set forth this new understanding in his *Critique of Pure Reason,* which constitutes one of the major events in the history of Western thought. The position taken was neither empiricist nor rationalist, but included basic elements of each. It is commonly called "the Critical Philosophy."

Kant sought to clarify the problem in terms of the different types of possible judgments. There are two basic distinctions here: that between synthetic and analytic judgments, and that between a priori and a posteriori judgments. A synthetic judgment is a statement or proposition in which the predicate adds something that is not in the subject. It "synthesizes" or joins something new to what is given in the subject. By contrast, an analytic judgment is one in which the predicate does not add anything new. It clarifies what is present in the subject, or, one might say, what can be learned by analyzing the subject. A definition would be an analytic proposition, for the predicate merely clarifies what is contained in the subject. There is no new knowledge, nothing is added. An empirical statement of judgment, on the other hand, is synthetic. If one reports that the population of a given city is 150 thousand persons, it is clear that something new is added by the predicate. No analysis of the concepts "population" and "city" can provide that information.

The distinction between a priori and a posteriori judgments focuses upon the relation of the judgment to experience rather than upon the relation of the predicate to the subject. An a posteriori judgment is one that is dependent upon experience, whereas an a priori judgment is one not dependent upon experience.

If knowledge is to be gained, it must be in terms of synthetic judgments, for, as noted, the analytic judgments only clarify or elaborate what is present in the concepts in the subject. It was generally understood that synthetic judgments were also a posteriori judgments, but Hume had shown (Kant believed) that we cannot gain knowledge (meaning certainty) by means of a posteriori judgments. This would mean that knowledge could only come by way of synthetic a priori judgments (Kant 1956, 41–62). How could this be?

In order to explain this Kant sought to determine the conditions necessary to account for experience itself. Stated in a general way, Kant concluded that we can only have even the simplest kind of everyday experience of the world around us if there is a combination of the given that we encounter in our sensations (the empirical emphasis) and activity on the part of the knower that organizes and interprets the multiplicity of sense impressions. It is not simply that there must be an "association of ideas" as with Hume. The knower makes a considerably greater contribution to experience than this (the rationalist emphasis).

Kant did not find it necessary to argue the point that we must receive sense data in order to experience the world. It evidently seemed clear enough to him that we do not in any way produce that data for ourselves. We receive it. But it also seemed clear to him that the reception of sense data, the vast miscellany of colors and sounds and tastes and textures, will not constitute our experience. By itself the many particular sense impressions could only confront us with a chaos, a kaleidoscopic confusion. Unless it is put into some kind of order, it will not in any sense be meaningful. One might suppose that this order is provided with the very reception of the sensations, that, for example, when I look into the woods I receive in one impression greens and blues and browns and grays, and thereby trees and sky and so forth. Kant held that it is a far more complex matter than this. Perhaps most obvious would be the fact that my experience of the woods also includes sounds such as the singing of birds and the rustling of leaves. It includes sensations of touch such as warmth and wind, and it includes subtle smells. How does all of this come together to constitute an experience of the woods? Will an "association of ideas" suffice?

Kant concluded that three distinct synthesizing activities must be recognized as necessary to account for such an experience. First of all, the sense data (Kant called them "intuitions") must be organized in terms of the general structures of space and time. We cannot have such experience if we have no sense of this being in front or behind, above or below, etc. Nor can we have experience if we have no sense of before and after. These are necessary structures. Our common assumption is that this is true enough, but hardly worth commenting on. Things are ordered in terms of time and space as we receive them. But Kant's judgment was that this is misleading. Our experience is always ordered in space and time, but why? He held that this is so, not because space and time are objective characteristics of the world "out there," but because the human capacity to have intuitions (to receive sense data) is such that it organizes—or, more specifically, "synthesizes"—the raw data in terms of these two ordering structures of space and time (ibid., 67–91).

The natural assumption would seem to be that we encounter space and time through sensation, but Kant argued that they could not be "read off" from our sensations in this way, because they are presupposed by all sense experiences. That is, space and time must be "there" already for us to have any sensations. Second, said Kant, space and time must originally be understood or given as infinite magnitudes. While one may formulate the words, it is not possible to have a concept of space that is limited, and the same with time. But it is also clearly impossible to have sense perceptions of such infinite magnitudes. Kant argued that the certainty of geometry is dependent upon this understanding of space as an organizing structure that "we" (our perceiving faculties) give to experience, for if our understanding of space were empirically derived we could not possibly know, for example, whether or not in some other "space" there might not be more than one straight line possible between two points (ibid.).

Kant called this first synthesizing activity, in which our very capacity to receive sense data organizes that data in terms of space and time, the "synthesis of apprehension in intuition" (ibid., 131). By itself, however, that would hardly yet constitute experience. To return to the example of experiencing the woods, it is not enough to have the many sensations ordered in space beside, or above, or behind one another, and so forth, and ordered in time so that I can calculate the movement of the branches, for example. The impressions in themselves are instantaneous. When I turn and look to the side or behind me, or when I blink my eyes, there must be something that enables me to relate the earlier impressions that I am no longer receiving to the ones I am now receiving.

The second synthesis that is required, therefore, to account for even simple experience is some activity involving memory. Kant called this the "synthesis of reproduction in imagination" (ibid., 132–33). The imagination must reproduce the earlier sensations in order that they may be "held together" with the present sensations. If this synthesis were not carried out, every instant of our lives would be precisely as if we suddenly found ourselves in a totally strange environment. There would still be only chaos, not experience.

Those first two syntheses are not yet sufficient, however, for there is thus far no understanding of those organized impressions. Until we *recognize* the organized impressions in some meaningful way, we do not yet have human experience. Kant called this third synthesis the "synthesis of recognition in a concept" (ibid., 133). If I say that I see trees and rocks and sky and that I hear birds and feel wind, I am "naming" things or labeling them. I am indicating thereby that I recognize them. The experience is meaningful to me. These names are learned during the course of experience. In Kant's judgment, however, there are fundamental structures of understanding that cannot be learned from experience because they alone make such recognizing possible. He called these fundamental structures of understanding "categories." Every human experience involves the use of four basic groups of categories, one of quantity, one of quality, one of relation, and one of modality. I see several trees, for example. Here I am using the category of *plurality* (one of the three categories of quantity). Or I experience the woods, rather than so many trees. Here it is the category of *totality*, which combines the categories of *unity* and *plurality*. These three are the more specific categories within the general category of *quantity*. In Kant's scheme there are four groups of categories with three in each group. He derived these twelve categories from the traditional table of logical judgments. The table is as follows:

1. Quantity
   unity
   plurality
   totality

2. Quality
   reality
   negation
   limitation

3. Relation
   subsistence-inherence
   causality-dependence
   community (reciprocity)

4. Modality
   possibility-impossibility
   existence-nonexistence
   necessity-contingency

In each of the four groups the third category is a combining of the first two. As totality is a kind of unity of a plurality, so also is limitation a kind of partial negating of the reality of something (ibid., 113–18).

What Kant was saying, then, was that these basic thought structures are prerequisite for any experience. We must employ them in order to understand whatever is being synthesized in terms of space, time, and memory. They are accordingly always present in human experience. The reason why they are always present is not because "things" "out there" are one or many substances existing within sequences of cause and effect, but *because that is the human way of recognizing sense impressions*. As H. J. Paton has pointed out, this whole structure of active synthesizing of the raw data of sense experience is analogous to viewing the world through a pair of blue-tinted glasses (Paton 1936, 1:166). If I wear such glasses, I will inevitably see a blue world. If I have always looked through such tinted glasses, I will assume that the world itself is blue rather than that this blueness is the result of the equipment through which I see. In a sense Kant has been describing the "equipment" through which we have experience. The general conclusion is that all of our experience is "conditioned" by our capacity to have experience. When one sees that point, it is suddenly very obvious, but it is difficult to see it in the first place. Because we always have experienced things in a certain way and have no way of escaping our own capacities for experiencing, we quite naturally assume that what we perceive is just exactly the way things are. One may say that that is the way they are *for us*, but that is quite different from saying that that is the way that they are *in themselves* or for other creatures or for God. I think of a desk first in terms of visual impressions. A person blind from birth has a partially different experience of desks. A spider, which has eight eyes and no doubt different structures of experience in all respects, certainly does not have an experience of "desk," though one may judge that in walking across my desk it is having some kind of experience. And what about God's understanding of such things? We simply cannot know. Given the traditional understandings of God, one may well say that God's understanding of a desk is far greater than ours, so much so that we simply cannot comprehend it. The point here is that it must be different, for we hardly suppose that God is limited by the structures of human sensation and understanding!

One of the immediate implications of this analysis of the necessary conditions of human experience, then, is that we do not experience things as they are in themselves. We only experience them in terms of our capacities for experiencing, and those are specifically human capacities. The one possible escape from this conclusion is to speculate that somehow things as they are in themselves happen to be identical with our way of experiencing them (or at least with our way of conceiving them) as a result of some sort of divinely preestablished harmony. There would be, however, no possible way of establishing such a speculative hypothesis, and it is difficult to see what would be the reason for trying—except that we would feel a bit more comfortable if we could continue the "common sense" supposition (Kant 1956, 174–75).

Thus far we have described three synthesizing roles that Kant held necessary for experience. First, the role of intuition in which sense data are not only received but schematized into a space-time manifold. Second, the role of imagination, which reproduces the impressions in order to hold experience together through the passage of time. Third, the role of the understanding, which recognizes these perceptions in terms of basic concepts called categories. This, Kant believed, would be sufficient to account for human experience, but he also indicated a fourth role. This is the role of *reason*, which seeks to pursue the synthesizing process to a complete unity. That is its nature, to seek unity. It does so in terms of three broad encompassing ideas: self, world, and God. The idea of self is one which brings all "inner" experience (our experience of our own willing, thinking, feeling, etc.) into a unity. The idea of world does the same for all of our "outer" experience. The idea of God then brings both self and world under an ultimate unity (ibid., 322–23, 557–609).

Kant held that these three ideas of reason are "heuristic fictions" (ibid., 614). By "heuristic" he meant to say that they are useful to us in our need for coherence, but by "fictions" he meant to say that we do not in fact have knowledge or any direct experience of such realities as the self, world, and God as projected by reason. Kant did not mean, for example, that there is no "self." He did wish to show (1) why every person has such an idea, (2) that nevertheless we do not have knowledge of such a reality, and (3) that careful examination of the (to him) traditional idea of the self as a simple, unitary, immortal substance showed this idea to entail serious logical difficulties (ibid., 328–51).

Without pursuing those specific discussions here, we may note the impact of Kant's analysis of experience upon these three ideas. Experience involves the reception and threefold synthesizing of raw sense data. (This is true also of "inner" experience, the only difference being that only time and not space is involved.) Those sense data, even organized in terms of the first two syntheses, are not meaningful unless recognized in terms of the categories. Those categories, on the other hand, are not structures of reality as it is in itself. They are rather the inevitable structures of human experience, for they are part of the "equipment" (the "blue glasses") through which we experience anything. Further, those categories taken by themselves are without any specific meaning. They are "empty" until they are filled with sense data. One of the best-known summary descriptions of the Kantian understanding of experience is thus: "Thoughts without content are empty. Intuitions without concepts are blind" (ibid., 93). Here again one may see the combining of the empirical and rationalist emphases.

When applied to the idea of the self, what he finds is that this idea is constructed from the categories without any sense content. It is an empty idea, for we never see or hear this substance ("substance" being one of the categories), though reason, ever seeking to unify experience, infers this reality as underlying all of our experiencing. But not only is the idea empty, it is constructed from the categories that are merely our way of synthesizing experience for understanding. We have no reason to believe that they can properly be applied to reality as it is in itself. Indeed Kant believed that he could show that they cannot apply to reality in itself, but that the effort to do so inevitably leads to antinomies or the affirmation of mutually contradictory propositions (ibid., 384–484).

To repeat, Kant was not arguing that there is no human subject, no real world, and no God. He was trying to show that our ideas of these realities are not legitimate and do not constitute knowledge.

Throughout this description of Kant's interpretation of human experience we have continually employed a distinction between reality as it is in itself, or things in themselves, on the one hand, and reality as we know it, or things as we experience them, on the other. This is a very basic distinction for Kant, and its shorter terms are "noumena," meaning things as they are in themselves, and "phenomena," meaning things as they are known in human experience. One may note an immediate difficulty. When Kant speaks of "things in themselves" or of "noumena" he employs the category of plurality, and he may be employing the category of substance. If instead he speaks, as he often does, of "the thing in itself," he is now using the category of unity. It has sometimes been thought that Kant was inconsistent in these shifting terms and in his use of the categories for speaking of "noumenal" reality. Actually, in his terms, this problem is inescapable, and it illustrates Kant's own contention. Of course we can only speak of "noumena" in terms of the categories that do not apply to them. That, he taught, is our only possible way of understanding. Thus we are always in difficulty in trying to refer to noumenal reality, particularly when we forget that our concepts are not applicable to it. Even here the "it" at the end of that sentence may be taken to imply that noumenal reality is singular. But on Kant's grounds, we simply cannot understand the noumenal, and our necessity of thinking in terms of quantity does not deny that, it illustrates it.

OUTLINE OF KANT'S EXPLANATION OF HUMAN EXPERIENCE

	Synthesis of apprehension in intuition	*Synthesis of reproduction in imagination*	*Synthesis of recognition in concepts*	*Search for unity*
things in themselves (noumena)	SENSATIONS			ideas of reason: self, world, God
	forms of intuition: space/time		concepts of understanding: the categories	
			EXPERIENCE PHENOMENA	
Intuition	Imagination		Understanding	Reason

How does all of this relate to the problem with which Kant began? In his judgment Hume had shown that scientific knowledge was only possible on the basis of synthetic, a priori judgments. But how could there be such judgments? Kant believed that the judgment that every event must have a cause was just such a judgment. But what could justify the confidence that that judgment is applicable to the world around us when it cannot be found in our experience of that world? Kant's answer lies in his conclusion that *our experience is not of noumena but of phenomena*. Science does not deal with things in themselves but with things as we experience them. The categories, including that of "causality-dependence," always necessarily apply to that experience, for they are inevitably an aspect of the synthesizing of that experience. We may be quite certain, therefore, that events which we observe are always subject to the judgment that every event has a cause. Science is quite secure, and we may have no doubt about its findings as we go about our daily tasks (Kant 1953, 52–84).

On the other hand, while science is quite secure, the result is quite different for metaphysics and theology. Metaphysics and natural theology have both assumed that the principle of causality applied to reality itself, to noumena. It is this assumption that makes possible inferences about God or any other proposed ultimate. But in Kant's interpretation of human experience the categories do not properly apply to such suprasensible realities. Neither inferences concerning the existence nor definitions of the nature of God or ultimate reality are possible for the theoretical use of human reason. This is not to say that we cannot offer speculative conjectures in which we employ the categories in an analogical or symbolic way, but it does rule out the possibility of *knowledge* in metaphysics and theology (Kant 1956, 565–66).

As one would expect, Kant was accused of denying the existence of God. Indeed it seems that whenever the possibility of proving the existence of God or of defining God's nature is denied, there will be a charge that God is being denied. This, however, is just careless thinking, and it is clearly not the intention or the result of Kant's analysis of human experience. It is clear from the whole course of Kant's writings that he believed in God, and that belief is quite consistent with his philosophy. But it was also his belief that the various efforts to prove the existence and define the nature of God were detrimental to human ethical responsibility and to the interests of faith. To either prove or define God, that is, to claim to have determinate theoretical knowledge of God, would be only to produce a false god captive to the limitations of human understanding. Kant said in the preface to the second edition of the *Critique of Pure Reason*, "I have therefore found it necessary to deny knowledge in order to make room for *faith*" (ibid., 29).

There is considerable reason to believe, however, that Kant was more concerned in these arguments with making room for morality than with making room for faith. Kant believed that if we could have certain knowledge of the existence and the will of God we would not be able to act morally. For Kant, to act morally was to choose freely to act in accordance with duty. If one acted from a desire for reward or from a fear of punishment, this would not be acting from respect for duty. To know the existence and will of God would inevitably, Kant believed, alter one's motivations to those hopes and fears of reward and punishment (Kant 1909, 245).

Morality could not, therefore, be defined as obedience to the will of God. It had to be clarified by the practical use of human reason. Kant also believed, however, that our moral experience, our experience of "the moral law within," only makes sense if there is a God who will ultimately provide happiness for the morally good (ibid., 220–23). That reasoning is not a "proof" of the existence of God. It is only an implication of moral experience *if* one chooses to believe that moral experience is not irrational. It is a conviction of the practical reason that provides nothing for the theoretical use of reason and no knowledge, in the strict Kantian sense of this term (ibid.).

Kant's philosophy, which like the others we have discussed included far more than has been mentioned in these sketches, has been enormously influential and has received a great deal of criticism. Neither he nor any other philosopher has had or will have the last word on philosophical issues. But, to whatever extent one may agree or disagree with Kant's conclusions, it remains true that he delineated both problems and possibilities that could not be ignored and that have changed the philosophical situation—and with it, the theological situation.

It may be argued, for example, that Kant established the irrefutable possibility that all human knowing is subject to a phenomenological limitation. Put differently, he demonstrated how it may be that we cannot have any knowledge (strict or definite or defined knowledge) of "things" as they are in themselves, but we are always limited by the ways in which our senses and our minds condition what we perceive and conceive. Kant thought he had proven this, but few would now agree. Nevertheless it follows that dogmatic claims concerning the nature of ultimate reality are not possible.

There has, of course, been no lack of theologians—from Kant's time to our own—who have talked and written as if they had a thoroughly intimate knowledge of the inmost being of God, all defined and organized by use of the categories of human conception, and proceeding on the assumption that God is also subject to the principle of causality. Even so, theology has been changed by Kant's work. The conviction that has been defended by some in every age of Judeo-Christian history that God is beyond human comprehension has been strengthened by Kant's work, and impetus has been given to the idea that theological statements are always in some sense "symbolic."

A particular point of influence has been in the understanding of what is meant by "revelation." It might appear at first that revelation is the answer to Kant, meaning that if God has given information about the divine will and nature, God would certainly have had the capacity to overcome the phenomenological limitation. If, for example, God has given the church to understand that God is one substance in three persons, then the church has a definite knowledge of the being of God, no matter what the epistemological difficulties may generally be.

But quite apart from the question of how one knows that it is God who has provided the church with such a doctrine, Kant's analysis of human experience inescapably applies to any supposed revelation also. God might indeed bypass intuition and put ideas into human minds. It remains the case, however, that if persons are to understand those ideas, they must be ideas that human minds can comprehend, they must be human conceptions. It is difficult to see how the strict application of human conceptions to God could fail to finitize God in a way unacceptable to faith.

The understanding of revelation predominant in Kant's time was the view that today is called "propositional," meaning that God miraculously gives us certain propositions or statements. Kant's arguments certainly did not rule this out altogether, but they did pose a most serious problem for those who sought to maintain the idea that any of these propositions gives literal knowledge of the being of God. One of the major influences of Kant's thought upon Protestant theology was accordingly a gradual but increasing turning away from the propositional understanding of revelation and developing of other ways of understanding the nature and meaning of revelation. In fact the distinguishing of propositional from nonpropositional interpretations of revelation is one of the major differences between what may loosely be called "conservative-orthodox" theologies on the one hand and "modern" theologies on the other.

The purpose of this chapter has been to introduce the revolution in philosophy that was precipitated by the revolution in science, to draw particular attention to the problem of knowledge that was central in these philosophical developments, and to note in a preliminary way the relevance of these considerations to theology. The success of the scientific revolution had shattered long-held convictions and broken confidences in traditional authorities, but it had also effected a new confidence in the human capacity to find truth.

The philosophers who grasped the significance of these developments sought to fill the gap left by the breakdown of traditional authorities and methods by developing the suggestions inherent in the general methods that were proving so successful in the sciences. The remarkable fruitfulness of the application of mathematics to the description of nature proved particularly suggestive of a rationalistic method which, presuming the applicability of the laws of reason to reality, saw in reason the adequate instrument for achieving knowledge. The scientific emphasis upon the data of observation and experimentation provided new impetus for the empirical emphasis in philosophy, which insisted that knowledge is basically dependent upon sense impressions. The rationalists, rather than arriving at any consensus in their efforts to draw forth a description of reality from reason, kept producing new and different interpretations, meanwhile ignoring for the most part the question of why they believed that the laws of reason were the structures of reality. The empiricists, on the other hand, kept discovering more and more difficulties in their efforts to explain how our experience is derived from sense impressions until Hume showed that a thoroughgoing empiricism leads to skepticism.

These two developments came together in Kant who acknowledged the responsibility of rationalism to justify its claim of the applicability of the laws of reason to experience and acknowledged reason's need for empirical data, while refusing to accept the skeptical conclusion of Hume's empiricism because of his conviction that the new science did in fact provide us with definite knowledge of nature. By interpreting human experience in terms of an interdependence of empirical data and rational ordering he was able to account for the applicability of the laws of reason to nature and to explain how science can provide certain knowledge, provided only that one recognize that this knowledge was of the phenomenal world and not of the noumenal. Science was accounted for, but human knowledge was severely limited, particularly in the realms of metaphysics and theology.

To whatever extent one may agree or disagree with these philosophies, it should be manifest from the foregoing summaries that citizens of the Occident were living in a new world among new questions, new problems, and new possibilities. Try as it might to ignore that new world with its questions about the problem of knowledge, theology would not long be able to avoid coming to grips with this problem if it was to remain in touch with the inhabitants of that new world.

WORKS CITED

Berkeley, G.
    1957
        A Treatise Concerning the Principles of Human Knowledge. Edited with Introduction by Colin M. Turbayne. Library of Liberal Arts, general editor Oskar Priest. New York: Liberal Arts Press.

Bréhier, E.
    1966   *The History of Philosophy: The Seventeenth Century.* Translated
                    by Wade Baskin. Chicago: University of Chicago Press.
Descartes, R.
    1901   *The Method, Meditations and Philosophy of Descartes.* Translated
                    by John Veitch. New York: Tudor Publishing Co.

    1950   *Discourse on Method.* Translated by Laurence J. Lafleur. Little
                    Library of Liberal Arts, general editor Oskar Priest, no. 19.
                    New York: Liberal Arts Press.

    1967   *The Philosophical Works of Descartes.* Translated by E. S. Hal-
                    dane and G. R. T. Ross. Vol. 1. Cambridge: Cambridge Uni-
                    versity Press.

Hume, D.
    1955   *An Inquiry Concerning Human Understanding.* Edited with In-
                    troduction by Charles W. Hendel. Library of Liberal Arts, gen-
                    eral editor Oskar Priest. New York: Liberal Arts Press.

Kant, I.
    1909   *Kant's Critique of Practical Reason and Other Works on the The-
                    ory of Ethics.* Translated by Thomas Kingsmill Abbott. 6th ed.
                    London: Longmans, Green & Co.

    1953   *Prolegomena to Any Future Metaphysics That Will Be Able to
                    Present Itself As a Science.* Translated with Introduction and
                    Notes by Peter G. Lucas. Manchester: Manchester University
                    Press.

    1956   *Immanuel Kant's Critique of Pure Reason.* Translated by Nor-
                    man Kemp Smith. London: Macmillan & Co.

Locke, J.
    1952   *An Essay Concerning Human Understanding.* In Great Books of
                    the Western World, editor-in-chief Robert Maynard Hutchins,
                    vol. 35. Chicago: Encyclopaedia Britannica.

Paton, H. J.
    1936   *Kant's Metaphysic of Experience: A Commentary on the First
                    Half of the Kritik Der Reinen Vernunft.* 2 vols. New York: Mac-
                    millan Co.

Russell, B.
    1945   *A History of Western Philosophy.* New York: Simon & Schuster.

3

THE
EVER-CHANGING
WORLD

Continuing
Scientific
Revolutions

THE SHAKING GIVEN the Western world view by the seventeenth-century scientific revolution was neither the last nor the most severe disturbance to come from the work of the natural scientists. The removal of humankind from the geographic center of the cosmos was a shock, but it did not prove too difficult to reestablish the human sense of being the highest and most important of God's creatures. That the universe was God's creation was not brought seriously into question, for while Newton's description of the orderliness of the great cosmic machine entailed a considerable reduction of the role of God within the cosmos, it also greatly encouraged natural theology. And it was human intelligence that, many believed, had discerned the laws governing the universe and that was now—in natural theology—providing knowledge of the reality and the nature of God.

Natural theology grew especially in the early eighteenth century, and was subject to severe philosophical attacks during the same century, as described in the previous chapter. Confidence in the finality of Newton's conclusions lasted much longer. Indeed, it was not until the last decade of the nineteenth century that the beginnings of a newer physics ended the unqualified dominance of Newtonian physics. The revolutions involved are considered below under "The New Physics." But some decades before these developments humanity's confidence in its own special dignity and certain bases of the belief in God came under most severe attack with the Darwinian revolution and the triumph of evolutionary theory.

EVOLUTION

The idea of evolution hardly originated with Charles Darwin; on any account it underwent a long process of development. Henry Fairfield Osborn traced some of its roots to the earliest Greek philosophers, though he also judged that the idea was not recognized as a whole until the work of Jean Lamarck (Osborn 1929, 3–4). Loren Eiseley says of the Comte de Buffon (1707–88) that he "managed, albeit in somewhat scattered fashion, at least to mention *every significant ingredient which was to be incorporated into Darwin's great synthesis of 1859*. He did not, however, quite manage to put these factors together" (Eiseley 1961, 39). There were very good reasons why one might not manage to put these ingredients together, for the prevailing convictions and orthodoxies were firmly opposed to any theory of evolution. The traditional Christian beliefs in the creation of all things in six days—with humanity existing in its fullness almost from the beginning—and in the account of Noah's ark preserving one male and one female of each species through a great earth-covering flood were still widely held, and it could be dangerous to contradict them. These beliefs entailed the further conviction that the history of the earth went back less than six thousand years, a period of time that would not allow for the evolution of species, and very few people had had the temerity to suggest much longer periods of time. Also persisting was a long-prevalent metaphysical belief in a creation whose perfection included the actuality of every possible level of being from pure Being (God) all the way down to the very edge of nothingness. In this view any gap would be an imperfection. This would require all species to have existed from the beginning, and it would not allow for some species becoming extinct.

Natural theologians and scientists also contributed to the antievolutionary convictions of the time. The principal argument of the former was that the marvelous way in which things in nature are adapted to ends shows that there must be a great Purposer who designed all things with ultimate ends in view. A theological explanation of nature remained dominant, and this was to be a point of particular conflict with the views of Darwin. At the same time, the scientific world was for the most part thoroughly committed to a belief in the fixity of species. Particularly influential in the eighteenth and early nineteenth centuries was the work of classifying species done by Carl Linnaeus (1707–78). As John C. Greene describes it,

> His lifelong ambition was to reduce the earth to order as Newton had the heavens. "God created; Linnaeus arranged" went an eighteenth century saying, and Linnaeus noted in his diary that his *System of Nature* was unique, "a work to which natural history has never had a fellow." In it, for the first time, every terrestrial production was assigned its place in one great system of classification. Nothing could have been more contrary to the idea of organic evolution than Linnaeus' aspiration to place every creature in its proper niche, yet the very effort to enumerate the species and genera definitively was to raise problems which could not be solved within the Linnaean framework. (Greene 1959, 131)

These problems were not immediately recognized, however, and though Linnaeus himself developed doubts regarding his own insistence that no new species can arise, he remained a powerful authority for that judgment (Eiseley 1961, 24–25).

Yet while these antievolutionary views remained dominant, evidence pointing toward a theory of evolution was accumulating. A. O. Lovejoy holds that available evidence in the fields of comparative anatomy, paleontology, biogeography, systematics, and animal and plant breeding was sufficient by 1812 to support several of Darwin's later conclusions, and that new evidence was discovered soon thereafter in several of these fields that fit only with evolutionary theory and rendered the prevailing hypothesis absurd (Lovejoy 1959, 356–414). This may well be true, but a satisfactory explanation of how the changes in species took place had not yet been offered, and this problem aided the power of long-held convictions to resist accumulating evidence. Also, the problem of time was more serious than might now appear, for under the scientific understandings of that time, there was no way in which the sun could have continued to burn throughout the immensely long period of time required by the theory of evolution.

This problem of time was quite basic. Ernst Mayr maintains that "the revolution began when it became obvious that the earth was very ancient rather than having been created only 6000 years ago. This finding was the snowball that started the whole avalanche" (Mayr 1972, 988). James Hutton (1726–97), sometimes called the founder of historical geology, showed that such phenomena as the appearance of boulders far from their evident places of origin, the deposits of sea shells far inland, and the stratification of the earth's crust could be understood in terms of the continuing effects of processes operating according to natural laws rather than by appeal to supernatural interventions. William Smith (1769–1839), a surveyor and engineer who spent many years working on the development of canal systems in England and making there systematic observations of the earth's strata, learned to identify the different strata by the distinctive fossils contained in them. This, taken together with the quite reasonable judgment that the lower a stratum was relative to other strata the older was its formation, constituted a principal clue to the history of life on earth. When joined with Hutton's conclusions about the long, slow but steady processes by which the formations of the earth's surface were developed, it implied an enormously long history of life moving through very gradual stages.

Georges Cuvier (1769–1832), founder of the science of comparative anatomy, learned by painstaking study and comparison of the bodily structures of different creatures how the various muscles and bones interrelated. He was eventually able to reconstruct reasonable likenesses of entire creatures from a few fragments. His studies demonstrated—on anatomical grounds—that the earth's living creatures could not all be placed on a single scale of increasing complexity and revealed that the earlier the stratum in which a fossil was found, the more the life forms detectable therein differed from now-living forms. This meant that the earth and life on it were much older than traditionally supposed.

Cuvier chose to explain his data by an expanded theory of "Catastrophism," according to which there had been several catastrophes rather than just the great flood, with new forms of life created after each one. Present forms of life were thus created after the last of these cataclysms. Cuvier believed that four such catastrophic events would account for the data. As further discoveries were made in fossil studies, however, it became necessary to continue increasing the number. Isaac Asimov, who calls Catastrophism "the last scientific stand against the theory of evolution" (Asimov 1964, 45), notes that some of Cuvier's followers postulated as many as twenty-seven catastrophes. But Catastrophism was not able to hold out indefinitely against the growing fossil data, particularly as this was marshaled by Charles Lyell in his *Principles of Geology* (1830). In particular, the evidence showed no point at which all of life was destroyed, but, quite to the contrary, it showed that there are living forms today that have existed throughout several periods alleged to have been terminated by the catastrophes (ibid.).

Various other discoveries during the first half of the nineteenth century were providing helpful clues. For example (1) Charles Lyell's extensive studies of ecology established the complex interrelationships existing among all living organisms and the great effects that could result from any change in the balance of an environmental situation (Eiseley 1961, 102). (2) Physicists discovered that one form of energy could be converted into another (Asimov 1964, 49). (3) Organic chemists discovered that "all species of living things were composed of the same classes of organic substances: carbohydrates, lipids, and proteins" (ibid., 54).

The chief problem that blocked the acceptability of a theory of evolution was the issue of the "mechanism" of change. Both Erasmus Darwin (1731–1802), the grandfather of Charles Darwin, and Jean Lamarck (1744–1829) had proposed evolutionary theories, and both had suggested that the change from one species to another could be accounted for in terms of the inheritance of acquired characteristics. This is the theory that as environmental circumstances change and create new problems the various creatures affected must make special efforts to bring about the changes in the species that are passed on to their offspring. At the same time, organs falling into disuse are

gradually lost. One of Lamarck's examples was the giraffe, which he argued
had developed gradually from a primitive antelope needing to stretch upward
for leaves for food (ibid., 40–41).

The idea of the inheritance of acquired characteristics has been shown to
have been an ancient and widespread belief (Eiseley 1961, 50), but its adop-
tion as an explanation of evolutionary change was rejected by the scientific
world—not only because of the general resistance to theories of evolution.
The evidence was against it, and none could be found that supported it (Asimov 1964, 41).

"Natural selection" as a chief ingredient in the answer to how evolution
takes place was a conclusion reached independently by two English natural-
ists, Charles R. Darwin (1809–82) and Alfred Russel Wallace (1823–1913).
Attention will be focused here upon Darwin, who reached the conclusion earlier, and whose name, for various reasons, is the one chiefly associated with
the success of evolutionary theory.

Darwin sailed as naturalist on the HMS *Beagle* in 1831 on a voyage that
was to last five years. Among the books he took with him was Charles Lyell's
Principles of Geology, which he studied carefully. This means that he was well
aware of the great age of the earth. He had been familiar with ideas of evolution since his youth. His diaries from the journey show that he had a keen interest in whether living species had indeed evolved and how this might have
taken place. His observations during the visits to many places provided evidence bearing on the former question. For example,

> He had become impressed, he informs us in the autobiography, "by the manner
> in which closely allied animals replace one another in proceeding southwards."
> He had come to see . . . a moderate amount of varietal distinction among animals
> upon a single time level and differing only in their geographical location. Such
> distinctions suggested quite powerfully the *local modification of a single species*,
> rather than the separate independent creation of a new form differing only in a
> quite moderate fashion, or in a few significant characters, from a previously ob-
> served species farther to the north. Later, this impression was to be powerfully
> intensified upon his examination of the Galapagos fauna. (Eiseley 1961, 161)

It was this visit to the Galapagos Islands that has received so much attention because it provided Darwin with a decisive clue to the mechanism of evolutionary change. After many pages describing his observations in these
islands, Darwin wrote in his journal of the voyage that he had failed to
recognize the most surprising natural feature of these islands until it was
pointed out by the vice-governor, Mr. Lawson. It was the fact that the tor-
toises from each of the different islands were different, sufficiently so that
Mr. Lawson could identify the island from which any tortoise brought to him

had come. Darwin wrote that it had never occurred to him that islands of the same composition, climate, and height, most of them in sight of each other, would yet show distinctive variations in the creatures that inhabited them. Such, however, he soon found to be the case (Darwin 1909b, 398).

> My attention was first thoroughly aroused, by comparing together the numerous specimens . . . of the mocking thrushes, when, to my astonishment, I discovered that all those from Charles Island belonged to one species (*Mimus trifasciatus*); all from Albemarle Island to *M. parvulus*; and all from James and Chatham Islands (between which two other islands are situated, as connecting links) belonged to *M. melanotis*. (Ibid., 399)

Darwin pointed out that it would not be nearly so remarkable if there were one kind of bird, lizard, plant, etc., on one island and quite different kinds on others.

> But it is the circumstance, that several of the islands possess their own species of the tortoise, mocking thrush, finches, and numerous plants, these species having the same general habits, occupying analogous situations, and obviously filling the same place in the natural economy of the archipelago, that strikes me with wonder. (Ibid., 401–2)

This data provided impressive evidence for the belief that the various species gradually develop (evolve), but there was still the question *how*. At the time of the voyage, Darwin had no satisfactory answer, and several years of study were to intervene before he was willing to propose an answer publicly. In the *Origin of Species* he described the problem and the supposition which stood in his way:

> But how is it that many of the immigrants have been differently modified, though only in a small degree, in islands situated within sight of each other, having the same geological nature, the same height, climate, etc.? This long appeared to me a great difficulty: but it arises in chief part from the deeply seated error of considering the physical conditions of a country as the most important; whereas it cannot be disputed that the nature of the other species with which one has to compete, is at least as important, and generally a far more important element of success. (Darwin 1909a, 423)

This emphasis upon the competition among the various species is the crucial idea that Darwin said in his autobiography was suggested to him by the reading of Thomas Malthus's *Essay on the Principle of Population*. Malthus's argument was that the human population always grows faster than does the supply of food, with the result that sooner or later the population must be reduced, perhaps by war, starvation, or disease. Darwin saw that this would also be true of all other species, and that the key factor in their competition for survival would be their relative strengths and weaknesses for obtaining food under their particular circumstances.

> For instance, those first finches on the Galapagos must have multiplied unchecked to begin with and would surely have outstripped the supply of seeds they lived on. Some would have had to starve, the weaker ones first, or those less adept at finding seeds. But what if some just happened to be able to eat bigger seeds or get by on tougher seeds or found themselves able to swallow an occasional insect? Those which were not possessed of these unusual abilities would be held in check by starvation, while those who could, however inefficiently, would find a new and untapped food supply and could then multiply rapidly until, in turn, their food supply began to dwindle. (Asimov 1964, 62–63)

This is Darwin's theory of "natural selection." The difference from the theory of the "inheritance of acquired characteristics" espoused by Lamarck is important. That theory argued that changes which develop during the lifetime of a creature due to its strivings could be inherited by its offspring. By contrast, the theory of "natural selection" holds that changes present at birth occasionally give the slightly different creature an advantage over its fellows in the struggle for existence. Thus, for example, in a situation in which tougher seeds were the only available food, those birds which *just happened* to have stronger beaks would be more likely to survive. Their number would increase while the previously predominant form would decrease and possibly be replaced altogether. Over a period of thousands of years many such occasional accidental advantages would occur, gradually increasing the degree to which a species would differ both from its ancestors and from descendants of the same ancestors who have been evolving in other circumstances.

This theory of "natural selection" does not explain why some creatures are born occasionally with differences from their parents, but only why some of these changes are maintained. That such changes occur had long been known by breeders who had selected the characteristics they had most liked in horses, sheep, and so forth. Darwin was now suggesting that such "selection" occurred "naturally," and that whereas breeders had never been able to continue their observations and selections over a long enough period of time to observe a change that could be seen as the appearance of a new species, "nature" had in fact had far more than long enough to accumulate such changes, as the geologists and the paleontologists had discovered.

In the *Origin of Species*, published in 1859, Darwin brought together a wide variety of arguments and observations in support of his theory of natural selection, but he almost completely avoided the question of the origin of human beings. The only reference is in the second to the last paragraph in which Darwin wrote:

In the future I see open fields for far more important researches. Psychology will be securely based on the foundation already well laid by Mr. Herbert Spencer, that of the necessary acquirement of each mental power and capacity by gradation. Much light will be thrown on the origin of man and his history. (Darwin 1909a, 505)

The question of human origin could not, however, be suppressed. It was the issue of greatest concern to the readers, and it was not hard for them to discern the direction of Darwin's thinking.

In 1871 Darwin published *The Descent of Man*, making explicit his belief in the inclusion of humankind within the whole evolutionary process and presenting his reasons. He pointed out, for example, that,

it is notorious that man is constructed on the same general type or model as other mammals. All the bones in his skeleton can be compared with corresponding bones in a monkey, bat, or seal. So it is with his muscles, nerves, blood-vessels and internal viscera. The brain, the most important of all the organs, follows the same law, as shewn by Huxley and other anatomists. (Darwin n.d., 395–96)

He also drew attention to such things as the intercommunicability of diseases between humans and other mammals, the sameness of method of reproduction, striking similarities in embryonic development, the vestiges of a tail (the coccyx), and various rudimentary organs and muscles (ibid., 396–410).

The inevitable opposition to this teaching was strengthened by the fact that at that time fossil evidence of the "missing links" between humans and their animal ancestors was not available. In 1838 Jacques Boucher had found crude axes whose stratum gave the first clear evidence of a much greater age of humankind than the "biblical" six thousand years, but, while relevant, this did not provide evidence that human beings had evolved from nonhuman creatures. The first Neanderthal skull had been discovered in 1856, but its significance had not yet been recognized. It was not until twenty years after the publication of *The Descent of Man* that the human fossil known as "Java Man" was discovered, and doubt as to the interpretation of these fossils persisted until the mid-1930s (Mayr 1963, 631). The paucity of human fossils and of human knowledge concerning them until very recently is illustrated by the success of the "discovery" in 1912 of fragments of a cranium and a jawbone together with fossil remains of extinct animals and implements of bone and flint in a gravel formation at a place called Piltdown Common in England. In spite of some objections, the fossils were long declared to be evidence of an ancient ancestor of humans. Many subsequent fossil findings and the development of newer techniques for the dating and chemical analysis of fossils led to the conclusion that "Piltdown Man" was a hoax. Someone had "doctored" and "planted" the evidence. This conclusion was not firmly established, however, until 1953. The lack of a fossil "missing link" in Darwin's evidence for the evolution of human beings has now, however, been supplied many times, and discoveries are still being made that continue to fill the gaps in our knowledge of our ancestry.

Another serious problem with the Darwinian depiction of evolution was the lack of understanding of heredity. The theory of "natural selection" presupposed the occurrence of occasional changes appearing inexplicably in the offspring which would then be maintained in their offspring. That this occurred was well known from observation. But how it occurred was not understood. For example, the common expectation in which Darwin shared was that the crossing of extremes would produce averages, such that the mating of a long-necked giraffe with a short-necked giraffe would produce a giraffe with a neck of medium length. This assumption, however, did not fit well with Darwin's theory that the better adapted are preserved.

The lack of understanding of the hereditary mechanism led, in fact, to Darwin's losing much of his confidence in the importance of natural selection and retreating toward a Lamarckian theory of the inheritance of acquired characteristics. Darwin was particularly impressed by the arguments of Fleeming Jenkin. As Eiseley summarizes,

> Fleeming Jenkin had, in actuality, well-nigh destroyed the fortuitous character of variation as it was originally visualized by Darwin. Jenkin set forth the fact that a newly emergent character possessed by one or a few rare mutants would be rapidly swamped out of existence by backcrossing with the mass of individuals that did not possess the trait in question. Only if the same trait emerged *simultaneously* throughout the majority of the species could it be expected to survive. (Eiseley 1961, 210)

As Eiseley points out, such simultaneous appearance of the change would require an explanation other than the natural selection of the occasional mutant. Lamarck's theory that the "germ plasm" is directly affected by environmental forces was one possibility. Another possibility was the theory of "orthogenesis" proposed by Karl Wilhelm von Nageli (1817–91). This is the view that evolution results from the force of an inner drive in a species. For example, he suggested that the fossil evidence that horses had developed from a dog-sized animal with four toes on each foot could be explained by the hypothesis that horses had an inner drive toward larger size and fewer toes (Asimov 1964, 74).

The beginnings of a modern scientific understanding of genetics are to be found in the work of Gregor Johann Mendel (1822–84), an Austrian monk who, for a while, was an amateur botanist. From 1857 until 1865 he made a meticulous study of pea plants. He very carefully cross-pollinated his plants in such a way that he was sure of the exact parent plants involved in the production of seeds. These seeds were then planted separately. In this way he discovered that seeds that are entirely from dwarf pea plants produced only dwarf pea plants, that is, that they are "true breeders." But he also found that this was not true of tall pea plants. Some were true breeders, and some were not. Further, when he crossed dwarf plants with true-breeding tall plants, they always produced tall plants, and when these tall hybrids were crossed, the results were mixed, being approximately one-fourth dwarf plants, one-fourth tall true-breeding plants, and one-half tall non-true-breeding plants. Mendel concluded that each plant had two factors for a particular characteristic, one from the male portion of the plant and one from the female portion. Thus when a true-breeding tall plant was crossed with a dwarf plant, each resulting plant would inherit one factor for tall and one for dwarf size. Then when these plants were crossed, the statistical probability would be that of four resulting plants (on average) one would have two tall factors, one would have two dwarf factors, and two would be mixed. This would account for Mendel's experimental results if it were further assumed that the tall factor is stronger than the dwarf factor, so that when the two are present together the plant will be tall rather than either dwarfed or middle-sized. Thus arises the distinction between dominant and recessive traits. One of the things he had demonstrated here was not only that crossing extremes does not produce averages, but also that characteristics—even if they are suppressed in a generation—are not blotted out. This would make it possible for random variations to reappear until natural selection could make use of them (ibid.).

When Mendel sent a written description of his observations and conclusions to Nageli (the botanist who had proposed the theory of orthogenesis), the latter responded negatively. Mendel, nevertheless, read a paper on his findings to the Brunn Society for the Study of Natural Science in 1865 and published his discoveries in 1866. Both of these presentations were ignored, and his tremendously valuable findings were lost until the beginning of the twentieth century.

One of the three persons who rediscovered Mendel's work about 1900 was Hugo de Vries (1848–1935), a Dutch botanist. During a period when evidence from physics seemed to show that the history of the earth could not be as great as Darwin's theories would require (because of the application of the law of conservation of energy to the possible "life span" of the sun before the discoveries of radioactivity and nuclear energy), de Vries was among those who began to look for evidence of evolution by jumps, so that the theory of evolution could be maintained in spite of the shortened estimate of the available time. He observed that wide differences had developed among some

American evening primroses that had but recently been brought into the Netherlands. Moving some to his own garden for close study, he found the same results that Mendel had observed in the pea plants. He also noticed that occasionally a markedly different variety would appear and would perpetuate itself over subsequent generations. He called these new varieties "mutations," and he believed that he had, in fact, observed evolution by jumps. Asimov points out that the kind of change de Vries had seen did not actually involve a change in hereditary factors, but notes that true mutations involving hereditary factors were soon observed (Asimov 1964, 79).

Indeed, mutations had previously been observed by herdsmen in the case of a short-legged sheep that had appeared in New England in 1791. This mutant was useful because the shortness of the sheep's legs made it incapable of jumping even low fences, and the change was bred and preserved (ibid.). Asimov goes on to note that herdsmen are usually not theoreticians, and it remained for de Vries to draw the scientific conclusions that were implied in such observations.

In 1900, de Vries, Karl Erich Correns, and Erich Tschermak von Seysenegg—all of whom had independently come to the same general conclusions —published their findings as corroborating the work of Mendel. The situation was now very different, for during the interim since Mendel's work a great deal more had been learned about cells and chromosomes, and their behavior in mitosis and meiosis had been discovered. Thus not only were Mendel's observations corroborated, but their basis was now explicable (Watson 1965, 16).

Another weakness in Darwin's theory had been removed. Of course, that did not settle all of the issues among the scientists, or even among the evolutionists, but further research continued to support and to clarify evolutionary theory. In particular, biologists continued to differ in the causal explanations that they preferred, until the 1930s when general agreement was reached on a synthesis of theories (Mayr 1963, 1–2). It is noteworthy that in spite of the vast amount of relevant knowledge that has since been gained, it can still be affirmed that "the current theory of evolution . . . owes more to Darwin than to any other evolutionist and is built around Darwin's essential concepts" (ibid., 2).

The impact of the Darwinian revolution has been enormous. Ernst Mayr speaks of it as "perhaps the most fundamental of all intellectual revolutions in the history of mankind. It not only eliminated man's anthropocentrism, but affected every metaphysical and ethical concept, if consistently applied" (Mayr 1972, 981). One might well ask why Darwin's work should have had so great an impact. After all, ideas of evolution were far from new and had been the subject of much discussion for quite some time. The answer lies in the effects of the concept of natural selection. Speaking generally, one may say that these effects were two: (1) the idea of natural selection made evolution both believable and persuasive; and, (2) the idea of natural selection basically changed the concept of evolution. It is these two things together that have had such wide-ranging implications.

As in the case of the issues raised by Copernicus and Galileo, there was no great disturbance as long as a few persons were discussing a hypothesis—that is, just speculation. However, as soon as a new understanding is presented as a scientific conclusion which—even if in a strict and narrow sense of the term it is not "proven"—makes sense of so much data and proves fruitful for so much further research that it is to be regarded as knowledge rather than speculation, the situation is fundamentally changed. Where basic convictions are at stake, the difference is comparable to that between a classroom debate and a life-and-death struggle. Darwin's theory of evolution in terms of natural selection was just of this sort, for it made sense of a great deal of data in several different fields, and it has continued to do so to the extent that it is the basic unifying theory underlying the many fields of modern biology and indeed most of the natural sciences. Whether evolution, including natural selection as a basic factor, is to be accepted is not a question in modern science. It is a given, a basic enabling conviction. It is, further, of very great practical importance to all of us, for evolutionary theory plays an important role in medical research, in the control of pests, and in agricultural science, to mention but a few examples.

Still, some argue that evolution is not a fact but merely a theory. This argument both manifests and creates confusion. As far as natural science is concerned, evolution is firmly established. It has been observed and manipulated. The word "theory" when employed here (never with the modifier "merely") refers not to evolution itself but to particular interpretations of how it takes place; as regards the details, new discoveries continue, and there are areas of uncertainty. This situation is much like that concerning gravity. The reality of gravity is not subject to doubt, but in the efforts to understand it there are "theories."

This scientific status of the theory of evolution would have serious implications for certain widely held traditional beliefs even apart from the concept of natural selection. It is, first of all, quite incompatible with biblical literalism and the understanding of creation that results from interpreting the Bible literally. Biblical literalism had been on the decline well before Darwin's time, since, among other reasons, it had been seen to be incompatible with the new astronomy established in the seventeenth century. As John Dillenberger points out, "The historical fact is that the defense of a literal Scripture began to crumble in England by the middle of the seventeenth century" (Dillenberger 1960, 111). Beginning to crumble and disappearing are, however, two very different things, and biblical literalism, which is still to be found among us today, was powerfully present in Darwin's time. It was not just the literalists who were threatened by the establishment of evolutionary theory, however, for that theory is also most difficult to harmonize with the doctrine of biblical inerrancy. Throughout the history of the Christian church, there has been far more support for the view that the Bible is without error (because inspired by God) than that it must all be interpreted literally. Indeed, one of the principal defenses of scriptural inerrancy has been the rejection of literalism, for that allows that whenever one passage appears to be in conflict with another or with knowledge otherwise obtained, it may be assumed that the supposed meaning of that passage was intended to be understood analogically, or allegorically, or symbolically, or poetically, etc. Such an approach may be employed to maintain the belief in biblical inerrancy in the face of the scientific acceptance of evolutionary theory, but it remains very difficult to avoid the conclusion that some biblical passages reflect an understanding of the origins of humankind and the other species that is quite other than that of evolutionary theory. Here, then, was another suggestion that even though the Scriptures may be "inspired," they show the humanness of their authors in the manifestation of the historically limited assumptions of another era and culture. This recognition of the historical nature of the Scriptures is one of the distinguishing characteristics of modern biblical scholarship. (See chap. 5.)

The challenges posed by evolutionary theory were greatly increased by the understanding of evolution in terms of natural selection. As Mayr has put it, "The result was an entirely different concept of evolution. Instead of endorsing the 18th-century concept of a drive toward perfection, Darwin merely postulated change" (Mayr 1972, 987). As long as evolution was viewed as progress or advance, it was easy to maintain the beliefs in the central role of the purposiveness of God and the primacy of humanity within those purposes. But the concept of natural selection eliminates both of these. It explains the observed developments quite without appeal to guiding purposes. This point *is* a matter of "theory," for the conclusion that the emergence of the "higher" species—including humankind—*can* be accounted for without hypothesizing divine guidance does *not* require the judgment that there is no role for God in that process, but it does allow for it. We can easily see today that science per se cannot deal with the subject of God, for the term "God" stands for a reality (so faith affirms) that transcends the limits of that which can be observed and tested experimentally. In Darwin's time this was—for historical reasons—less clear, so the theory of natural selection was perceived as a denial of God and of any purpose in human life.

Just how disturbing this was is reflected in a series of quotations gathered by R. N. Stromberg in *An Intellectual History of Modern Europe*. He quotes George Bernard Shaw as saying that "if it could be proved that the whole universe had been produced by such selection, only fools and rascals could bear to live." He notes that the German scientist Von Baer indignantly rejected a theory that reduced humans to being "a product of matter" and debased them to the level of animals, and that Adam Sedgwick, professor of geology at Cambridge, said that if accepted the theory would "sink the human race into a lower grade of degradation than any into which it has fallen since its written records tell of its history" (Stromberg 1966, 278–79). But as Professor Huxley so dramatically pointed out to Bishop Wilberforce in 1860, the question here was not one of what we want to believe, but one of truth.

The seventeenth-century scientific revolution had removed the earth, and thus humankind, from the geographic center of the cosmos, and it had minimized the assumed role of God in the movements of the cosmos, but it had left a role for God and even provided a new basis for belief in God in terms of the Great Designer of so impressive a machine, and it had left humans free to see themselves as the central purpose for which that machine had been created. Evolution by natural selection appeared to reduce humanity to the status of but another animal that came to be quite by chance, and at the very least seemed drastically to reduce such roles as had been left to God. To begin with, it removed "God" from science. As Mayr points out concerning the situation before Darwin's work, "It became a moral obligation for the scientist to find additional proofs for the wisdom and constant attention of the Creator." Perhaps even more important, "To a greater or lesser extent, all the scientists of that period resorted, in their explanatory schemes, to frequent interventions by the Creator (in the running of His world)" (Mayr 1972, 983). Both of these mixings of science and theology are seen today as utterly inappropriate to the work of the scientists.

But "God" has not just been removed from the practice of natural science. It is not only that evolution by natural selection left no place for divine interventions in the phenomena that it described, but that the resulting understanding of life as a purposeless struggle for survival in which one kind succeeds at the expense of another, many species becoming extinct, and in which future environmental changes may be expected to terminate humankind also, seems incompatible with belief in God. Darwin came to this conclusion, saying, "I cannot persuade myself that a beneficient and omnipotent

God would have designedly created the Ichneumonidae with the express intention of their feeding within the living bodies of caterpillars, or that cats should play with mice" (Stromberg 1968, 102). There was (and is) also the general problem that when the arguments that have been used in support of belief in God come under serious attack, it always appears that belief in God is equally under attack with them. As noted earlier, belief in God had been confidently asserted by appeal to the argument from design in the world. Now the most impressive instances of this alleged design had been explained without any need for the Designer. Natural theology suffered another serious blow from the success of Darwin's theory of evolution. But so also did appeals to the authority of church and Scripture. Apart from the fact that to appeal to those authorities as a basis for believing in God is to argue in a circle (since the presupposition of those appeals is that they have been given their authority by God), certain of the authoritative teachings of the churches and supposed teachings of the Bible had now been shown to be in error. The appeal to miracles as evidence for the reality of God also suffered as a result of the success of evolutionary theory, for the trend toward common belief that all events are ultimately subject to scientific explanation—a trend that began in Europe at least as early as Galileo's work—was given a great boost by that success.

Of course it remained possible to argue that even if science could provide an entirely "godless" account of the development of all present forms of life, it could not account for the existence of that from which these forms had evolved. Even if today we may have reasonable hypotheses about how the universe developed into its present shape and how life emerged from inorganic origins, the question still remains about how one may explain the existence of that from which all of this could develop. This is not a form of the familiar "God of the gaps" argument, for properly understood it does not introduce God as a hypothesis to fill a gap in current scientific knowledge. It points rather to an ultimate question. That, however, is all that it can do. To assert that there must be a God to explain the origin of that from which the universe has developed is only to move the problem very slightly. Of course, the theologians have long since pointed out that to speak of God as the origin of all existing things is not the same as suggesting that the elephant which may once have been believed to hold up the earth stands on the back of a great tortoise, for "God" is not a term referring to another finite and temporal reality, but includes within its meaning that God cannot not be. One may, however, grant that this is part of the meaning of the word "God" without concluding that the appeal to God is required by the question of the origin of all existing things. In either case (with or without the affirmation of the reality of God) there is for the human mind a mystery: why is there something rather than nothing? Even granting that if God is, no origin of God's being is needed, it still remains a mystery for the human mind *that* God should be rather than that nothing should be. If the evolutionary theorist chooses to believe that there is no answer to the question of why there should have been that from which the universe has developed, he or she is not being less rational than one who believes that God is the answer to this question.

Another possible approach is to appeal to the need for God's role at certain decisive points within the evolutionary developments. Probably the most likely point here is the first appearance of life. On any account this was a remarkable occurrence, and it cannot be accounted for by appeal to natural selection, for that is a process that presupposes life. Believing that it is the teaching of modern science that the beginning of life on earth was a matter of sheer chance, Pierre Lecomte du Noüy, writing in 1947, sought to show that such a happening is so grossly improbable as to be unbelievable. He calculated that the chance occurrence of even one of the molecules necessary for the appearance of life would require 10^{243} billions of years (that is, 1 followed by 243 zeros). But hundreds of millions of such molecules would be necessary, so, he concluded,

> events which . . . *need an infinitely longer time than the estimated duration of the earth in order to have one chance, on an average, to manifest themselves can, it would seem, be considered as impossible in the human sense.* (Du Noüy 1947, 35–36)

The fact that du Noüy estimated the age of the earth at only two billion years whereas it is now calculated that life itself has been on earth longer than that does not seriously affect his argument. Yet, du Noüy's argument has not been found persuasive because modern science does not teach that either biological or life-preceding processes on earth operate by sheer chance. One of the experiments that has encouraged scientists in the belief that it will become possible to give a thoroughly satisfactory biochemical explanation of the origins of life on earth was conducted by S. L. Miller some five years after the publication of *Human Destiny*. Taking account of the current calculations as to the probable makeup of the earth's atmosphere prior to the appearance and evolution of life, and of the fact that a great deal more of the sun's ultraviolet rays would have reached the earth's surface prior to the development of the ozone layer above the earth, he sought to simulate the effects of the sun's energy on that atmosphere by sending an electric charge through a mixture of gases and water believed to replicate the primordial circumstances. Within a week organic compounds including some of the amino acids had appeared (Asimov 1960, 204). If so much can happen in a week, is a billion years too short a time for the given chemical processes to produce simple life? Scientists certainly did not think so.

Subsequent experiments using varying chemical mixtures have had similar results, but they have not been able to move very much farther toward a full explanation of the development of life. For various reasons, some scientists in the 1980s have argued that an explanation of that development that focuses more on the geochemistry is more likely (Cairns-Smith 1985, 90ff.). Nevertheless, the Miller experiments revealed the error of du Noüy's argument, and the scientific world is firmly convinced that the origin of life was a natural evolutionary process.

The questions concerning the origin of life are to be distinguished from those about the processes of its subsequent evolution. At the time of Miller's original experiment (1953) even the complexity of the problems was not yet well understood, but that was also the year in which the structure of DNA was solved, giving birth to another revolution in biology and to the specialized field of molecular biology. It is now known that DNA is the molecule containing the genetic information that guides the reproduction of species, and it is also now understood how RNA, a chemically similar nucleic acid molecule, conveys that genetic information to bring about the syntheses of protein molecules that largely constitute the new organisms. These discoveries, along with the solving of the "genetic code" and the discovering of the structures of some protein molecules, took place during intense and highly competitive research throughout the 1950s and 1960s. The importance of these developments in relation to continuing doubts about evolution was underscored by Jacques Monod, who explained,

> that while all thoughtful, hardheaded biologists believed in the neo-Darwinian theory of evolution, and although it was clear that that was the only one that gave a rational description of how evolution could have happened, yet it was *still* true that that theory was profoundly incomplete so long as did not also have a physical theory of heredity. Since the whole Darwinian concept is based on change through the inheritance of new traits, on selection pressing on a somewhat varied population, so long as you could not say exactly how inheritance occurred, physically, and what the generator of variety was, chemically, Darwinism was still up in the air. (Judson 1979, 217)

The developments in molecular biology have answered these questions, and neo-Darwinism is no longer "up in the air." The molecular biologists have been able not only to understand but also to manipulate the inheritance of mutations.

The origin of life on earth is another matter. It has been established from the fossil record that one-celled organisms were present on the earth more than three and a half billion years ago. Since the environmental circumstances were very different then (for example: no competing living organisms, no free oxygen in the atmosphere, no ozone layer and therefore strong ultraviolet rays from the sun), there is no possibility of observing the same natural development today. Many details of ways in which life could and may have come to be on earth are now understood, however, and a fully satisfactory explanation is expected.

The appearance of life and certain other events such as the emergence of human beings are regarded by some scientists such as Theodosius Dobzhansky and Teilhard de Chardin as representing what we might call "qualitative leaps" in the evolutionary process, but not as unbridgeable gaps. As Dobzhansky explains concerning the evolution of human beings,

> the point which the believers in unbridgeable gaps miss is that the qualitative novelty of the human estate is the novelty of a pattern, not of its components. The transcendence does not mean that a new form of unity has come into existence. At all events, no component of the *humanum* can any longer be denied to animals, although the human constellation of these components certainly can. (Dobzhansky 1967, 58)

This does not mean that God has nothing to do with the coming to be of humankind, but it does mean that God is not an appropriate hypothesis in a scientific explanation of that emergence. It is also a reminder that here again believers in God would be wise to avoid another "God of the gaps" argument. That strategy of defending religion against the real or supposed threats of advancing scientific explanations by introducing "God" as an explanation wherever science has not yet produced one has provided a long series of embarrassing reversals. Sooner or later the scientific explanation has been forthcoming, and because a supposed argument for the reality of God has been eliminated thereby, it has appeared, once again, that God's reality was rendered less likely.

The direct challenge of evolutionary theory to theology has not, however, been in terms of the question of whether God is, but rather of how we should understand God's activity. Modern evolutionary theory is not in itself incompatible with belief in God, but it may be judged to be incompatible with some ways of understanding "God's actions." Indeed, this may be said of modern science in general, the development of evolutionary theory only having made this particularly evident.

In the prescientific understandings of reality in the Western world it was commonly assumed that God and other supernatural powers played direct causal roles in daily events. Illness would be seen as punishment from God or attack by an evil spirit. The defeat of the Spanish Armada was interpreted by both sides as resulting primarily from the actions of God. Such a world view is basically incompatible with modern science and its achievements. It has been a fruitful assumption continually corroborated in modern science that natural events can be entirely explained in terms of natural causes. Certainly human choices constitute a factor other than natural law, and human beliefs, commitments, and prayers affect human choices, but this does not introduce God as a cause displacing any of the causal factors otherwise constituting an adequate explanation of events.

Prior to the success of Darwinian theory, scientists were themselves using "God" as an explanatory hypothesis to fill many gaps in their understandings of life. Evolutionary theory filled so many of these gaps with natural factors that today the scientific community would not contemplate using "God" to cover any of the remaining questions (of which there are many).

There are, obviously, many persons today who are quite willing to try to live in both the prescientific world and the modern world. Theologians, however, cannot afford the luxury of such careless thinking and self-deception. Contemporary theology has been forced by evolutionary theory and by modern science in general to struggle with the understanding of the activity of God in a way quite different from the situation facing the theologians who developed the familiar traditional ways of understanding Christian faith. One of the most natural assumptions of those earlier theologians cannot be maintained today unless one is prepared to reject the very bases of modern science and couple with that rejection the assumption that God has so designed the creation as to deceive systematically the practitioners of modern science. One does not have to be a theologian to recognize that this last assumption is blasphemous.

The resulting theological problem of how we are to understand the activity of God in the world is one of the more basic issues of contemporary theology, and it not only differentiates contemporary theology from earlier theologies, but it also distinguishes contemporary theologies from each other. Some of the ways in which theologians have dealt with this problem, seeking to elucidate the active role of God in the world apart from causal intervention, will be discussed in a subsequent volume.

What should be clear at this point is that the scientific success of evolutionary theory has significantly changed the beliefs of modern persons and has confronted Christian theology with serious questions and the need for reformulation.

THE NEW PHYSICS

The Darwinian revolution has hardly been the only modern scientific development requiring serious change in humanity's understanding of its world. Indeed, some of the most basic concepts in terms of which people have sought to understand the world—the concepts of space, time, matter, motion, and causality—have had to be reinterpreted as a result of "the new physics," especially the developments associated with the concepts of "relativity" and "quantum."

The impact of these developments upon theology has thus far not been comparable to that of evolutionary theory, perhaps because the relevance of the new physics for theology is mediated by its philosophical implications that continue to be subject to debate. Even so, several questions have been raised in this way that should be noted here.

It is not possible to explain relativity theory, quantum physics, and related concepts in several pages, primarily because these developments constitute an understanding of physical reality that does not "fit" the conceptual possibilities that common language provides. One might reasonably expect this to be only a temporary problem, since the meanings of words undergo continual change, and scientific discoveries have often had the gradual effect of changing the common understandings of words and of experience itself. In the case of the new physics, however, there are special problems.

The general understanding of physical reality that was developed on the basis of Newton's synthesis gave, for the most part, a very adequate account of the normal range of human experience—and it still does. It is only as the searching of scientists has reached beyond that normal range of human experience that Newtonian (or classical) physics has been found to be inadequate. In both the larger world, the world of astronomy in which distances and velocities quite beyond normal human perception are involved, and the small world, the atomic and subatomic world dealing with sizes too small for normal human perception, the expectations built upon classical physics have proved to be wrong. What has been found has not been fully explicable in the concepts of classical physics. Indeed, much of what modern physical research has concluded is not imaginable. That is, we are incapable of picturing the nature of reality as modern physics finds it to be. Physicists must deal with it by means of complex mathematical formulas. Those not so trained find themselves in a situation roughly analogous to that of a tone-deaf person trying to appreciate the beauty of a symphony.

During the two centuries in which Newtonian physics held sway, physical reality came to be understood as a machine whose parts were made up of atoms or corpuscles, the location and velocity of which were exactly determinable. Just as one can exactly predict the future activities of a machine when all of its parts, movements, and forces are known, so also in the mechanistic universe were all future events believed to be entirely determined and therefore, in principle, predictable. Perhaps the best-known statement of this is from Laplace:

> An intellect which at a given instant knew all the forces acting in nature, and the position of all things of which the world consists—supposing the said intellect were vast enough to subject these data to analysis—would embrace in the same formula the motions of the greatest bodies in the universe and those of the slightest atoms; nothing would be uncertain for it, and the future, like the past would be present to its eyes. (Capek 1961, 122)

Space provided the context within which every particle of reality could be located and was interpreted always without question in terms of Euclid's geometry. Time was not regarded as of great importance and was itself commonly understood in terms of space, as in the drawing of time lines. Matter was thought of as "an impenetrable *something*, which fills completely certain regions of space and which persists through time even when it changes its location" (ibid.). Its basic elements were believed to be beyond change or destruction. Motion, being a change in the location of matter in space, required the concepts of space, time, and matter, but it was not derivable from them. According to their definitions space, time, and matter were quite incapable of accounting for motion. Only motion could account for motion, and its quantity in the universe must remain constant. It was believed that there are such things as "absolute motion" and "absolute rest" as measured against the fixed structure of space. Causality was understood in terms of the mechanical determination reflected in the quotation from Laplace. All of this provided a sense of certainty and security in a very rational, very understandable, very dependable universe. In fact, so much seemed to have been explained that there was widespread belief among physicists that there was little yet to be discovered.

One of the areas in which difficulties developed for the mechanistic interpretation of reality was the study of light. It was long believed that light is propagated instantaneously, as common experience suggests. But the Danish astronomer Olaf Roemer established that light has a finite velocity and approximately determined that velocity in 1676. Newton explained this traveling of light as the movement of particles that are so small that they can travel through such things as air and glass—a mechanistic explanation. Christian Huygens suggested the alternative theory that light is propagated by waves rather than particles. Eventually very careful experimentation showed the wave theory to account more adequately for such light phenomena as interference. But if light is a wavelike movement, there must—from a mechanistic standpoint—be a medium for these waves such as air provides for sound waves. This supposed medium was called "ether," and was believed to be an extremely fine substance filling all of space.

The existence of such a substance should be detectable by careful experimentation. The many experiments that were devised for this purpose all had negative results, however. For example, if there is such an ether, then light traveling in the same direction as the earth's movement should have a slightly different velocity from light traveling at right angles to that direction. The famous Michelson interferometer experiments designed to show this difference failed to do so. Subsequent experiments have had the same result.

Albert Einstein (1879–1955) judged that the experiments were correct, that there is no ether, and that the velocity of light in a vacuum is the same in all directions within any uniformly moving frame of reference. The abandoning of belief in the ether, which was indicated by the failure of all of the experiments seeking to detect it, was also a giving up of the mechanistic interpretation of nature. The conclusion that light is propagated with identical velocities in all directions within every uniformly moving frame of reference (or every coordinate system) had very strange results from the standpoint of classical physics. In that traditional way of understanding reality *time* had an absolute meaning, and therefore so did such notions as "simultaneity" and with it the concepts of "sooner" and "later." But it is now found—in the special theory of relativity—that two events that are simultaneous for an observer within one coordinate system are not simultaneous for an observer outside that system. To most of us this seems absurd. We feel that the illustrations of this conclusion must involve some kind of trick, for "we know" that two events either are simultaneous or they are not. At the very least one of those two observers must see things "as they really are," while the other is somehow misled. This is the absolutism of classical physics—and of "common sense." But Einstein's special theory of relativity teaches that the most that can be said is that the events are simultaneous for all observers within the one coordinate system but are not simultaneous for the observers in the other system. There is no absolute time framework.

That traditional supposition of absolute time and absolute simultaneity was based first on the belief that light is propagated instantaneously. This would mean that when we look at the sky on a clear night we see all of the stars as they are right now. When it was discovered that light has a finite velocity, it was believed that we could calculate just how long ago the light we now see was emitted from each star and that these calculations would be valid for all possible observers in the universe. This assumed that the velocity of light could be added to the velocity of the earth and the stars just as any mechanical velocity could be added. This is what is denied by the special theory of relativity and the experimental evidence on which it is based. Because—as a matter of experimental observation—light travels (in a vacuum) with identical velocity in all directions within a uniformly moving frame of reference, there can be no such absolute time and simultaneity for observers in differently moving frames of reference.

In addition to absolute time, absolute space is eliminated by this discovery. The idea of an absolute spatial context for everything in the universe is repudiated not only by the denial of the ether which supposedly provided that context, but also by the recognition that location in space cannot be separated from specification in time. In classical physics space and time could be readily abstracted from each other so that an object's spatial location was entirely determinable without regard to time. The special theory of relativity shows this to be quite impossible. There cannot be an absolute spatial context without the absolute simultaneity which has been found not to be.

The "fusing" of space and time that comes with the special theory of relativity has sometimes been misunderstood as reducing time to a fourth dimension of space. It is this that gave rise to ideas of traveling into the past. Actually it is more accurate to speak of this fusion as a temporalizing of space than as a spatializing of time, though space and time remain qualitatively distinct from each other. The basic point is, though, that while they may be distinguished from each other, they are now seen not to be separable. This fusion, together with the recognition that there is no absolute space or time (or even an absolute time-space), constitutes a major shift in humanity's understanding of its "world."

In addition to new understandings of time and space, the special theory of relativity has also brought a change in the understanding of matter due to a change in the understanding of one of its most fundamental properties, *mass*. Mass is the property of resisting change of motion. In classical physics it was a firm conviction that the mass of any body is fixed and unchanging. Einstein was able to infer from the tenets of the special theory of relativity that mass increases as velocity increases. This is not discernible with velocities observed in normal experience, but only as velocity approaches that of light. Einstein's equation for this increase of mass with velocity, which has been thoroughly verified, indicates that if a body could exceed the velocity of light its mass would be infinite. This is one of several reasons in relativity theory for the conclusion that no material body can attain a velocity greater than that of light, though some particles do reach more than 99 percent of the velocity of light.

The discovery of the relation of mass and velocity led Einstein to the further deduction that energy has mass. It is the relationship of energy to mass that is expressed in the famous formula $E = mc^2$ (energy equals the mass [in grams] multiplied by the square of the velocity of light [in centimeters per second]). The practical importance of this deduction has been graphically illustrated by the development of atomic weapons and power. Its theoretical impact has also been enormous. It had previously been firmly believed that energy and matter are two fundamentally different kinds of being, whereas it is now seen that they are but two forms of the same reality.

One of the implications of this interchangeability of mass and energy is that the energy of light has inertial mass. This explains why the path of light is curved in a gravitational field. This is an aspect of the *general* theory of relativity in which Einstein was able to extend the theory beyond the limitations of the special theory. Whereas the latter applies only to inertial systems in uniform motion, the general theory is applicable to nonuniform motions and thus to all coordinate systems. In this general theory Einstein gave a new interpretation of gravitation that was able to account for certain astronomical phenomena that had been inexplicable in terms of the Newtonian theory. Another aspect of the general theory of relativity is its conclusion that the universe cannot be properly understood in terms of Euclidian geometry as Newton's system assumed.

The general theory of relativity has not been as fully verified as the special theory. It was, however, able to account for a previously inexplicable deviation in the orbit of the planet Mercury, and it predicted phenomena, such as the effect of gravity upon light, which had not been previously seen or suspected. It effectively explains the present relevant findings of science, and new experiments continue to support it. Thus, while it may be said to be open to theoretical question, it is not now under serious attack.

It should be evident even from these oversimplified descriptions that the fruitfulness of relativity theory has brought basic change to the understanding of physical reality. Relativity theory has not, however, been the only source of such changes, and perhaps not even the greatest. The physicist-philosopher Werner Heisenberg (1901–76) has said that "it is in quantum theory that the most fundamental changes with respect to the concept of reality have taken place" (Heisenberg 1958, 28). The same point is made even more emphatically by the physicist Louis de Broglie (b. 1892) who wrote,

> despite the importance and the extent of the progress accomplished by physics in the last centuries, as long as the physicists were unaware of the existence of quanta, they were unable to comprehend anything of the profound nature of physical phenomena, for without quanta, there would be neither light nor matter and, if one may paraphrase the Gospels, it can be said that without them "was not anything made that was made." (Broglie 1953, 14)

Here again, as with relativity theory, the normal range of human experience is not what is immediately involved. In the case of quanta, it is atomic and subatomic phenomena that are under consideration. The belief in immutable atoms as the smallest units of reality and therefore the ultimate constituents of all things was an ancient conviction that fit well with the mechanistic character of classical physics. When electrons as fantastically smaller components of atoms were discovered in the last decade of the nineteenth century, it appeared for a while that these could simply take the place that had previously been given to atoms as the basic fixed particles of reality, and the mechanistic world view could continue undisturbed.

Problems became evident, however, in the study of radiation from heated bodies. To their surprise researchers were unable to develop a formula that would indicate how the energy radiating from a heated body varied with the temperature and the wavelength. In addition the data obtained from spectroscopic studies of the radiation of heated black bodies did not correspond with the conclusions required by the classical assumptions. In 1900 accurate measurements of the heat spectrum were made. Max Planck (1858–1947) then succeeded in specifying a mathematical formula for these measurements which showed that energy was emitted from the radiating atoms in *distinct quantities*. That is to say, he concluded that the emitted energy did not vary in a continuous flow from less to greater, but by tiny "jumps." This is commonly illustrated by comparison with a monetary system such as that of the United States in which the amount of a price or a payment cannot be subdivided further than a penny. With a shift to Italian lira, one can determine an amount in much smaller divisions, but in either case there is a minimal quantity in the monetary system, and all transactions must be in multiples of this specific quantity.

What Planck's formula suggested was that, analogously, in certain phenomena energy cannot vary continuously but only by discrete quantities or "quanta." Planck's efforts to reconcile his conclusions with the understandings of heat in classical physics failed, and he quickly recognized that the quantum hypothesis had revolutionary implications. This became even more evident when Einstein extended that hypothesis to other forms of energy. He applied it, for example, to the puzzling photoelectric effect in which electrons are emitted from a metal plate when a beam of light falls on it. It had been discovered that the intensity of the light beam could be varied without any change in the energy of the ejected electrons. That energy did vary, however, in relation to different light frequencies (colors). If the light source is far away and very dim, the number of electrons emitted is less, but the reaction is still instantaneous and the energy of each electron the same. These experimental findings were not consistent with the supposition that light is a continuous stream of energy. Einstein applied the quantum hypothesis, proposing that light should be understood as composed of many individual "packets" of energy. He called these "photons." The ejection of an electron would result from its being struck by a photon whose individual energy would be the same even when the beam of light was less intense. Planck's formula showed how to calculate that energy in relation to the frequency.

This new interpretation of light as composed of quanta ("bundles") of energy was in sharp contrast to the accepted understanding in terms of waves which is required in order to account for the diffraction of light and the patterns of interference. These two understandings of light are incompatible, but each accounts for experimental data that the other does not explain.

Further research showed the fruitfulness of quantum theory for the understanding of the action of electrons in the atom. But just as in the case of light, it was found that electrons must sometimes be understood as waves and sometimes as particles (quanta).

One conclusion that was becoming ever clearer in the development of quantum physics was that atomic and subatomic phenomena cannot be properly defined or described in the terms borrowed from those things that we can directly observe. A further illustration of this fact was the discovery that we cannot simultaneously have an accurate determination of both the position and the velocity of an electron. The more accurately velocity is specified, the less accurately can position be determined, and vice versa. Heisenberg clarified the formula for the uncertainties involved, and this is accordingly known as Heisenberg's Uncertainty Principle or Principle of Indeterminacy.

A common illustration of both the uncertainties regarding the position and velocity of quanta (electrons or photons) and the wave/particle dualism is found in experiments in which a beam of light is focused on an opaque screen with two tiny slits in it (or a beam of electrons similarly focused on a metal screen with two such slits) with a photographic plate placed behind the screen. The beam of electrons or photons produces a series of bands or dark areas alternating with light areas on the photographic plate. These dark areas are made up of tiny marks produced by the individual electrons or photons, the marks being clustered to produce the darkening with only an occasional mark appearing in the light areas between the dark bands. The individual marks are readily interpreted by the understanding of electrons and photons as quanta or particles, but the distribution of those marks in bands makes sense in terms of the understanding of the beams as waves. It has also been established that if a single electron could be projected at the screen, the probabilities regarding its point of impingement upon the photographic plate would be altered by there being two openings in the screen rather than one.

Presumably a single electron could pass through only one of these openings such that if it were properly understood as a particle, there would be no influence from the fact of the second opening.

Physicists are able to work effectively with calculations of the statistical probabilities even though they cannot remove the uncertainties regarding the particular quanta. But how is one to understand the nature of the realities under study?

One approach offered by Niels Bohr (1885–1962) is called the Principle of Complementarity. Stated in somewhat oversimplified terms, this is the view that even though neither "wave" nor "particle" is an accurate depiction of electrons (or photons) and in spite of the fact that those two descriptive models are mutually incompatible, it is nevertheless necessary and fruitful to develop and describe experiments in terms of *both*. The findings and understandings made possible by each one are "complementary" to those of the other. Taken together they give us both greater understanding and a reminder of the limited character of that understanding. One factor that has encouraged this view that the apparently contradictory methods of description are actually complementary is that different forms of mathematical symbolism used to describe the experiments can be transformed into each other even though one was developed in terms of waves and the other in terms of particles.

The limitations referred to here are partly epistemological (that is, having to do with our knowledge) and partly ontological (having to do with the realities of which we seek knowledge). First of all, the concepts with which we seek to understand things are drawn from common everyday experience involving things that we can perceive, whereas electrons are far too small to be observable even with the aid of microscopes. Our "natural" assumption that all of reality must fit these concepts is challenged here, the judgment being that elementary "particles" are neither wavelike nor particlelike and that they cannot properly be said either to have or not to have location. These terms are appropriate to observables but not to the subatomic realm.

The size factor involved has the further effect of magnifying the influence of the instruments of observation upon what is observed. If we seek to determine the temperature of a pail of water, the thermometer we use changes that temperature, but ordinarily to so small a degree as to be negligible. In experiments designed for the study of electrons the effects of the instruments are not negligible. They introduce an inevitable range of uncertainty into the findings. This degree of uncertainty is written into the equations by which statistical probabilities are determined for the atomic events.

No one interpretation of the findings of atomic physics has been acceptable to all physicists. There has, in fact, been a great deal of debate among physicists about how the uncertainties in the experimental data of quantum physics should be interpreted. Do they just arise from the inappropriateness of the traditional concepts, and if so can we remove the apparent contradictions and the uncertainty factors by developing new concepts? Or is it that we are confronted by a temporary limitation in our knowledge that we may expect to be overcome by further scientific developments that will remove the apparent contradictions and uncertainties? Or is it rather that science has come here upon matters that are inescapably beyond the reach of precise human knowledge? This would mean that the uncertainties of our knowledge cannot be removed, and that therefore we can never know whether there is an indeterminateness in nature. Beyond all of these positions that attribute the peculiarities of quantum physics to limitations of human knowledge there is the firm conviction of some physicists that we are confronted with clear evidence of *indeterminateness in nature* as well as uncertainty in human knowledge.

The most basic point of concern here is whether nature turns out in its very roots to be indeterminate, that is, whether there is a degree of randomness in atomic and subatomic events. Even though only the last of the foregoing interpretations attributes such indeterminateness to nature (rather than attributing it entirely to human ignorance), all of those interpretations leave room for this possibility. Even those who insist that this appearance is due entirely to the limits of human knowledge are expressing a belief and perhaps a hope, for the acknowledgment that we do not know admits the possibility of that randomness in nature. At the very least this means that the confident affirmation of thoroughgoing natural determinism that was characteristic of classical physics is not compatible with the current state of knowledge in that science. On the other hand, this shift does not represent a denial of the regularities and predictabilities of the larger-scale natural occurrences with which classical physics was concerned. Here one deals with large aggregates of photons, electrons, atoms, etc., which are dynamically related to each other in such fashion that the impossibility of making such predictions about any particular electron does not make such predictions impossible for the aggregate. Various extreme suggestions about the implications of indeterminacy have resulted from a failure to recognize this point.

This simple sketch of some aspects of quantum physics will hardly provide an understanding of that science, but it should make possible the recognition that here again, as in the case of relativity theory, the findings of modern science have required a significant change in the understanding of the world that was so firmly held during the two-hundred-year dominance of Newtonian or classical physics. The concept of matter as consisting of fixed and unchangeable minimal units, an idea already repudiated by the discovery in relativity theory that mass and energy are interconvertible, has been found to be incompatible with discoveries concerning the nature of electrons and other "elementary particles." The same research has raised serious questions about the thoroughgoing determinism that had been judged to be characteristic of nature. It has also shown the concepts with which we have sought to interpret physical reality to be inadequate, as is graphically illustrated by the wave/particle duality and the inapplicability of our conception of "location" to electrons. These findings have in turn suggested that the ultimate nature of physical reality may not be fully comprehensible to human understanding.

This last point does not imply that science will not learn and understand more than it knows today. Indeed, it is to be expected that there will be a continuing increase in the understanding of physical reality, and one may well expect further scientific "revolutions." Present interpretations in relativity and quantum theories may have to be modified, though this does not imply any basis for the hope that classical physics will be reinstated. One of the many abandoned beliefs of that outmoded physics was the confidence that the human intellect can completely comprehend physical reality. It may seem rather paradoxical to say that in knowing more science has a more humble view of its capacity to know, and that while science can be expected to continue increasing its knowledge indefinitely, it is nevertheless limited in the degree of exact comprehension that it may be expected to attain. Nevertheless, these are not contradictions. For example, the discovery that both "wave" and "particle" conceptions are needed while neither is adequate was both an increase in knowledge and a recognition of a limit to comprehensibility. When one considers that present knowledge of physical reality shows it to have an "eventlike" character, a character of dynamic becoming, rather than the characteristics of static things, it should be evident that full comprehension is not possible, because we can now see that there is openness in nature's future. A further limitation is apparent in the fact that continuing scientific learning reaches even farther beyond the range of human perception, and while one may not be willing to go as far as Kant's judgment that concepts without percepts are "empty," it seems hard to deny that they are lacking in clarity.

Taken together then, relativity and quantum physics have repudiated or basically changed every fundamental concept of the understanding of physical reality that dominated physics in the eighteenth and nineteenth centuries. The degree to which this is so is, in fact, far more profound than this discussion has been able to show. The question arises here as to just what relevance, if any, all of this has for theology.

Unfortunately, from the standpoint of students of theology (including professional theologians), it is not possible to conclude that the new physics is either irrelevant for theology or of simple relevance. Nevertheless, both of these judgments may be found in the work of theologians today, implicitly and explicitly. The judgment of irrelevance is present implicitly wherever theologians simply ignore these scientific developments and the questions they raise. It is present explicitly when, for example, theologians continue to assert that theology deals with the infinite and the eternal on the basis of divine revelation, whereas science can deal only with the finite and the temporal on the basis of human perceptions. Apart from the fact that theologians who suggest this thorough separation are finally unwilling to keep their theologies that unrelated to the world in which we live, it may be noted that the very statement of the contrast employs concepts that have been changed by the new physics.

The idea of simple relevance has been suggested in several ways. For example, some have concluded that indeterminacy in quantum physics vindicates their belief in human moral freedom against the determinism of classical physics (Mascall 1956, 195–201; Rust 1967, 232ff.). Others see indeterminacy as providing a place for divine intervention without interruption of natural law (Griffin 1973, 99; Wells 1962, 41–85). Others have suggested that recent theories in astrophysics (which have not been discussed here, but which are closely related to the theories we have sketched) that argue that the universe can have had only a finite history give support to the belief in the divine creation of the universe (Pius XII 1952; Wells 1962, 106ff.). Although one cannot deny relevance of these theories in physics to the theological doctrines, these are, nevertheless, oversimplified inferences. The principle of indeterminacy and the theories about the origin of the universe are open to debate and to varying interpretations. The physical determinism of classical physics need not be interpreted as denying human moral freedom. The indeterminacy in atomic and subatomic events does not deny physical determinism in larger-scale events and is therefore a dubious basis for affirmations concerning divine intervention. Such considerations are intended here only to illustrate the questionableness of leaping quickly from affirmations in physics to affirmations in theology.

Questions concerning human freedom, divine activity, and the origin of the universe are, of course, important for theology, and theologians cannot reasonably ignore such findings of science as may be relevant to these questions. The point being made here is that the relationships between the fields of natural science and theology are not simple but complex, and the issues involved in relating the two are always subject to debate. Whenever we see theological conclusions drawn directly from natural science, we should examine the reasoning with care, for it is likely that it harbors misunderstanding.

Nevertheless, there is at least one clear and direct point of relevance of modern physics to theology. The findings of modern physics are not compatible with biblical literalism. It seems to be commonly supposed that the battle about evolution being fought by some very conservative Christian groups hinges entirely upon one's acceptance or rejection of a neo-Darwinian interpretation of evolution by natural selection. Although that continues to be a focus of sometimes heated dispute, it is by no means the only point at which the biblical literalists are in conflict with modern science—even on the issue of evolution. Modern physics (nuclear physics, quantum mechanics, astrophysics, etc.) has found that the universe itself and the matter and energy of which it is constituted have evolved, and a remarkable amount of this process has now been explained. It is a process that has taken some twenty billion years since the massive explosion that initiated its still-continuing expansion. There is room for argument about aspects of that statement, and more is being learned every year. One of the conclusions that is not subject to scientific dispute is that the history of the universe has extended over many billions of years. Biblical literalism cannot accept this conclusion. The simple fact of the matter is that biblical literalism is incompatible with *all* of modern natural science, and not just certain "theories" in biology, for the natural sciences are deeply involved with one another. They do not and they cannot function independently. (As will be explained in chapter 5, biblical literalism is also incompatible with the *social* science of historiography, but that is not our concern here.)

The greater, though indirect, relevance of the new physics for theology lies in its general characteristics rather than its specific teachings. This relevance may be illustrated briefly in terms of (1) the historical relativity of human concepts, (2) the increasing recognition of problems of language and meaning, (3) the importance of the problem of knowledge, and (4) the growing strength of a new conceptual framework for philosophy and theology.

1. The first point is the most obvious and is the basis in this context for the other three. The attempt has been made in the foregoing sketches of the new physics to show that the findings of that science have required fundamental reinterpretation of our concepts of time, space, matter, motion, and causality. These foundation stones for any understanding of nature and the universe were understood in very largely the same way in both classical physics and the "common sense" of the era of that physics. Inevitably those concepts were presupposed in the theologies of that era. Whatever we seek to understand and interpret, whether it be "matter" or "God," we must do so with the

help (and hindrance) of the concepts that are a basic component of our cultural setting, the concepts in terms of which we have learned to think. We may find our inherited concepts to be inadequate and seek to change or replace them. Much of the history of philosophy consists of such efforts, and the same has been true in major events in the history of natural science. The efforts to bring about such conceptual changes are, however, most difficult, for we must work from within the very conceptual framework that we seek to alter or replace. What is illustrated here that is important for students of theology to recognize is that even the most basic concepts with which we try to understand are historical developments reflecting the limitations of particular human settings and experiences. That is, human concepts are historically and culturally relative. They and their meanings change from age to age and from one cultural context to another.

This fact has enormous implications for theology, which is a human activity carried on with human concepts. It requires the recognition that if we wish to understand the teachings of the theologians of any other era or culture (thus including the biblical teachings) we must pay the price of a major effort to grasp the different conceptuality that was being presupposed. The "translation" involved here is much more difficult than a substitution of the words of one language for those of another.

Also required is the recognition that the way in which a theological problem was posed and "solved" in another era and/or cultural setting may be so much the result of the conceptual limitations of that context as to be of questionable validity now. Questions have been raised, for example, concerning the hallowed doctrines of the Trinity and of the two natures of Christ. How are we to grasp today what was meant by the fourth- and fifth-century Greek and Latin words for "person," "substance," and "nature"? Is it possible that we have other and (for us) better conceptual tools today with which to deal with the church's struggle to understand God and Jesus Christ? These are not simple questions, but it is now much clearer than in earlier periods of Christian theology that they are possible and necessary questions.

Certainly the new physics has not itself posed such theological questions. What it has done is to provide a particularly graphic and—for our time— impressive illustration of the historical and cultural relativity of human concepts and of human language in general. Our era is so deeply impressed by the accomplishments of the natural sciences that it has been more willing to acknowledge the inadequacy of traditional concepts demonstrated by the physicists than to hear the same general point from philosophers, historians, and theologians.

2. The new physics has also illustrated another limitation of language

besides its historical and cultural relativity. The wave/particle dualism has shown that there can be circumstances in which our languages are simply incapable of giving adequate direct expression to what is, nevertheless, "known." The "knowing" in this case is not a full and clear comprehension. The understanding is limited, for our capacity to understand is limited by our language. Whether the limitation in this case is one that can be overcome by the development of new concepts, or whether it is a limitation that human conceptuality cannot surpass remains subject to debate. In either case the present fact demonstrates the limitations of language in a useful way. Various theologians, philosophers, and poets have recognized such limitations for millennia, but under the impact of the success of the natural sciences in recent centuries there has been a growing tendency to believe that if something could not be stated clearly, it might well be meaningless. Natural science itself must now repudiate such a narrow view of language and meaning.

Of course, the fact that the physicists may find it necessary to speak of electrons sometimes as particles and sometimes as waves, while also holding that they are neither particles nor waves, does not validate any theological metaphors or paradoxes. It does, however, demonstrate to an age impressed by science that metaphorical, paradoxical, and other nonliteral modes of speech may be most appropriate for some subjects. It would seem strange to acknowledge that the structure of an atom cannot be described literally or directly and yet to insist that God can be!

The importance of the problems of language and meaning for theology has in varying degrees been recognized throughout the history of Christian theology (and in the Scriptures). There has, however, been far more attention to these problems in this century than previously, and natural science has been but one of several contributing influences.

3. In discussing the relativity and the limitations of human concepts and language, we have been touching upon the problems of knowledge. Science is, in general, an effort to increase human knowledge. There have been periods in the history of science during which scientists have been able to ignore what philosophers call the epistemological problem, but major scientific revolutions commonly raise questions about human knowledge. As explained in chapter 1, they were raised by the beginnings of modern science in the seventeenth century, because the methods employed by scientists involved a basic change from the previously dominant beliefs as to how we can gain knowledge. Natural science itself came to provide the models for theories of knowledge, though this process did not produce general agreement. Some emphasized the mathematical aspects of science and taught that reason is the principal instrument of knowledge because it has an inherent capacity to

grasp the nature of reality. These rationalisms were generally supportive of natural theologies that sought to show that human reason can attain knowledge of the existence and nature of God. Others focused upon the empirical aspects of science, its dependence upon sense experience in observation and experiment, and taught that all human knowledge is grounded in sense experience. The general tendency of the developing analyses of empirical knowledge was toward increasing doubt regarding the possibility of reaching metaphysical or theological knowledge. Kant sought to show that sense data and reason must collaborate to constitute human experience, but that this recognition entails the further conclusion that all human knowledge is limited by the very way in which we know, so that we can never know "things as they are in themselves," and we cannot reach knowledge of reality itself or of God. Natural theology was ruled out by the conclusion that whether it begins from empirical data or from human reasoning it cannot claim to begin from the real. The experience is qualified by the human way of experiencing, and the reasoning is simply an expression of the given character of human understanding. There is no way for either to describe reality itself properly. The idea that revelation gives us knowledge of God was also rejected in Kant's thinking. Here again the same human concepts would have to be employed, concepts which even if they were somehow applicable to God would have no clear meaning (would be "empty") because there would be no sense data to give them content.

Although Kant's work had a major impact upon the work of various theologians, giving rise to redefinitions of revelation, epistemology has continued to be more an area of debate than agreement. Science continued to gain knowledge of the world by the use of both reason and empirical data without concern whether that knowledge was (in Kant's terms) noumenal or phenomenal. The general impact of its success upon Western culture has been to produce an increasing though not well-defined empiricism and a decreasing interest in metaphysics and theology.

These epistemological questions have again been forced upon scientists by the developments of relativity and quantum physics. Empiricists have been impressed by the fact that it was empirical data that revealed the limitations of classical physics and led to the new theories. Rationalists find support in the remarkable capacity of mathematics to reveal rational harmony in the new findings, noting that mathematics is a construct of human reason. What the new physics means for the Kantian is a complex question. It seems clearly to have shown that Kant's conviction that we must always understand in terms of a specific set of concepts (categories) is mistaken. The new physics has changed some of our basic concepts. In like manner Kant's firm beliefs in the necessity of Euclidian geometry and Newtonian physics have been shown erroneous. It would not be easy today to find a supporter of Kant's belief in synthetic, a priori truths. We simply do not have the kind of utterly certain knowledge that Kant believed Newton's physics to provide.

On the other hand, Kant's basic point that human knowledge is always limited by our particular human capacities to perceive and to understand has not been shaken at all by the scientific developments. One might be misled by the physicists' debates as to whether indeterminacy is a characteristic of reality or only of the limits of human knowing, but this is not Kant's distinction of "things in themselves" and "things as we know them." If future discoveries in physics settle that question about indeterminacy, the knowledge gained will be knowledge of phenomenal reality, for it will be partially comprised of and qualified by human perception and conception.

What the new physics has done with respect to problems of knowledge is to provide an emphatic reminder that those problems remain unsolved— even by the spectacular successes of natural science. In addition, relativity and quantum physics have added impressive evidence to the arguments of the philosophers against naive realism. Naive realism is in effect the belief that there is no problem of knowledge, because our common experience is direct knowledge of the real as it is in itself. Relativity and quantum physics have found the understandings of reality derived from that common experience to be inadequate when the range of experience is extended, and the atomic realm is found to be so utterly unlike the things of common experience that we cannot even imagine it. What this says to students of theology is that they can ignore the problem of knowledge only at the risk of remaining naive in their theological judgments.

4. In addition to these epistemological considerations, the impact of the new physics upon theology is to be seen in the growing school of theology called "Process Theology." The several theologians who belong to this group (including John B. Cobb, Jr., Lewis S. Ford, David Griffin, Peter N. Hamilton, Ralph E. James, Jr., and Schubert M. Ogden) are seeking to reformulate Christian doctrines and the meaning of "God" in general by use of a new conceptual framework developed in "Process Philosophy." It would be misleading to suggest that the new physics is the sole impetus for this development, but it has been one of the important originative factors. This influence is explicit in the work of the mathematician and philosopher Alfred North Whitehead (1861–1947), the principal fountainhead of contemporary process thought. Arguing in part that modern science has shown reality not

to be constituted basically by enduring substances as was assumed in traditional science and metaphysics, he developed an essentially different interpretation of reality in which it is understood to have the character of "energy," "process," or "event." This "philosophy of organism," as Whitehead called it, is difficult to understand primarily because it seeks to make this fundamental change in our basic concepts. Our everyday experience is still—for the most part—readily understood in the traditional concepts, and this fact reinforces the power of those concepts over our understanding. It is not surprising, however, that many persons with considerable training in modern physics are attracted to process thought, for it clearly "fits" better with the findings of relativity and quantum physics and helps one to see why this new physical knowledge seems so strange and is so difficult to comprehend.

Traditional theologies have been formulated with the traditional conceptualities. The effort to reformulate those doctrines, or rather the meanings those doctrines sought to express, in a basically different conceptuality opens up great creative potential for theology. One should note, however, that such a new conceptuality opens up theological *possibilities,* not *necessities.* That is, there will be a growing number of ways found in which such a new conceptual scheme can be employed by theologians, just as the more traditional concepts were used in many ways theologically. There is also, of course, more than one philosophical development of process thought, and one must expect newer ones to arise. The possible effects of the development of process thinking upon theology will accordingly be themselves in process of development for a long time.

The same must be said for the possible impact of the new physics upon theology. That impact is for the most part yet to be felt, and it is likely that further important implications are yet to be seen. Even so, the graphic illustration of the historical and cultural relativity of human concepts, of the limitations of language, and of the continuing importance of the problem of knowledge, together with the rise of process thought as a conceptual framework attuned to the newer understandings of physical reality, show that the new physics adds another dimension to a world today that is profoundly different from the worlds in which the various traditional Christian orthodoxies were formulated.

Both evolutionary theory in biology and relativity and quantum theories in physics show not only that humankind may be expected to reach continually newer understandings of the experienced world, but also that that world is an inherently dynamic and developing one. It should hardly be surprising that in such a context theology must be in a continuing process of reformulation.

WORKS CITED

Asimov, I.
1960   *The Wellsprings of Life.* Signet Science Library. New York: New American Library.

1964   *A Short History of Biology.* American Museum of Science Books. Garden City, N.Y.: Doubleday & Co.

Broglie, L. de
1953   *The Revolution in Physics.* Translated by Ralph W. Niemeyer. New York: Noonday Press.

Cairns-Smith, A. G.
1985   "The First Organisms." *Scientific American* 252, no. 6: 90–100.

Capek, M.
1961   *The Philosophical Impact of Contemporary Physics.* London: D. Van Nostrand.

Darwin, C.
1909a   *The Origin of Species.* Harvard Classics, vol. 11. New York: P. F. Collier & Son.

1909b   *The Voyage of the Beagle.* Harvard Classics, vol. 29. New York: P. F. Collier & Son.

n.d.   *The Descent of Man.* Modern Library. New York: Random House.

Dillenberger, J.
1960   *Protestant Thought and Natural Science.* Garden City, N.Y.: Doubleday & Co.

Dobzhansky, T.
1967   *The Biology of Ultimate Concern.* Perspectives in Humanism, edited by Ruth Nanda Anshen. New York: New American Library.

Eiseley, L.
1961   *Darwin's Century: Evolution and the Men Who Discovered It.* Garden City, N.Y.: Doubleday Anchor Books.

Greene, J. C.
1959   *The Death of Adam: Evolution and Its Impact on Western Thought.* Ames: Iowa State University Press.

Griffin, D. R.
1973   *A Process Christology.* Philadelphia: Westminster Press.

Heisenberg, W.
1958   *Physics and Philosophy: The Revolution in Modern Physics.* World Perspectives, edited by R. N. Anshen, vol. 19. New York: Harper & Brothers.

Judson, H. F.
1979   *The Eighth Day of Creation: Makers of the Revolution in Biology.* Touchstone Book. New York: Simon & Schuster.

Lovejoy, A. O.
    1959   "The Argument for Organic Evolution Before the Origin of
                    Species, 1830–1858." In *Forerunners of Darwin, 1745–1859*,
                    edited by B. Glass, O. Temkin, and W. L. Strauss, Jr., 356–
                    414. Baltimore: Johns Hopkins Press.

Mascall, E. L.
    1965 [1956]   *Christian Theology and Natural Science: Some Questions in Their
                    Relations.* Hamden, Conn.: Shoe String Press.

Mayr, E.
    1963   *Animal Species and Evolution.* Cambridge: Harvard University
                    Press, Belknap Press.

    1972   "The Nature of the Darwinian Revolution." *Science* 176 (June
                    2, 1972): 981–89.

Noüy, P. L. du
    1947   *Human Destiny.* New York: Longmans, Green & Co.

Osborn, H. F.
    1929   *From the Greeks to Darwin: The Development of the Evolution
                    Idea Through Twenty-Four Centuries.* New York: Charles Scrib-
                    ner's Sons.

Pius XII, Pope
    1952 [1951]   *Modern Science and God.* Translated by P. J. McLaughlin.
                    Dublin: Clonmore & Reynolds.

Rust, E. C.
    1967   *Science and Faith: Towards a Theological Understanding of Na-
                    ture.* New York: Oxford University Press.

Stromberg, R. N.
    1966   *An Intellectual History of Modern Europe.* New York: Appleton-
                    Century-Crofts.

    1968   *European Intellectual History Since 1789.* New York: Appleton-
                    Century-Crofts.

Watson, J. D.
    1965   *Molecular Biology of the Gene.* New York: W. A. Benjamin.

Wells, A. N.
    1962   *The Christian Message in a Scientific Age.* Richmond: John
                    Knox Press.

4

THE STRANGE NEW WORLD WITHIN

The Depth-Psychological Revolution

PERSONS OF THE "Western world" have had their understandings of themselves and their world subjected to repeated challenges since "the Copernican Revolution" denied us our supposed place at the center of the cosmos. No threat to our assumptions about ourselves, however, has been more direct or more profound that that of the depth-psychological revolution begun by Sigmund Freud. Here it is not our place in the cosmos or our lineage or our claims to knowledge that are reinterpreted, but our very thoughts, feelings, and motivations. For many reasons there has been far less general acceptance of these new views than those of the natural scientific revolutions, but it would seem hard to deny the accuracy of Lionel Trilling's comment on the influence of Freud:

> The effect that psychoanalysis has had upon the life of the West is incalculable. Beginning as a theory of certain illnesses of the mind, it went on to become a radically new and momentous theory of mind itself. Of the intellectual disciplines that have to do with the nature and destiny of mankind, there is none that has not responded to the force of this theory. Its concepts have established themselves in popular thought, though often in crude and sometimes in perverted form, making not merely a new vocabulary but a new mode of judgment. (Jones 1963, ix)

The name "depth psychology" is broader in meaning than the term "psychoanalysis" which refers to the more specifically Freudian theories. Depth psychology, as Ira Progoff put it, is "the study of man and all that pertains to him in terms of the magnitude of the human personality and the dimensions of experience that underlie and transcend consciousness" (Progoff 1956, 23). Thus it includes those many theories which hold that there is much more to the psychic life of persons than what is conscious to them or can readily become so. Indeed, according to these views, conscious thought, feeling, and experience constitute only a small part of our mental life (using the word "mental" in a way that does not restrict it—as is commonly done—to consciousness). Human being cannot be understood until major attention is given to its "unconscious depths," a phrase that seeks to employ the analogy of additional *dimensions*. The suggestion is that just as it would be impossible to understand a house in terms of height and width without the third dimension, depth, so also is it impossible to comprehend human beings without recognition of unconscious psychic factors profoundly at work.

By contrast, the fields of medicine, psychiatry, psychology, philosophy, theology, and in fact the whole cultural outlook of Freud's time were dominated by the assumption that persons are to be understood primarily in terms of their capacity for conscious reasoning. This assumption has indeed characterized the history of Western thought and remains common today. This is hardly surprising, for apart from the threatening character of the depth-psychological theories and the consequent defensiveness, it is by the nature of the case extremely difficult to offer persuasive arguments for the reality of "the Unconscious" when any evidence must necessarily be in the realm of consciousness. It is even most difficult to *explain* what is meant by "the Unconscious," since the explanation and the understanding must be in the realm of consciousness and are therefore different in kind and inappropriate—to some degree—to the meaning sought.

The attempt will be made here to suggest the general depth-psychological meaning of "the Unconscious" by tracing some of the factors that led Freud to his conclusions and then by looking at some of the major differences that developed early in the movement, particularly in the work of Adler and Jung.

The idea of the Unconscious did not originate with Freud. Robert I. Watson notes attention to unconscious psychological phenomena in Plato, and he points out various other treatments throughout the centuries, including several before Freud in the nineteenth century. But, he concludes, it was Freud who discerned the vital role of unconscious motivations and opened them to systematic study and to therapy (Watson 1968, 459).

The question of whether or not Freud discovered the unconscious is roughly analogous to the question whether or not Columbus discovered America. Whether first or not, it was Columbus who opened the Americas to Europe, and Freud who opened the unconscious for Western society.

SIGMUND FREUD

Sigmund Freud (1856–1939) was trained and practiced as a medical doctor working particularly in neurology, the study of the nervous system and its illnesses. It was primarily his desire to understand phenomena he encountered in human illnesses that led him to his then very unorthodox theories and methods of therapy.

The crucial first steps were developed by Freud's close friend, Dr. Joseph Breuer, and one of his patients in what has come to be known as "the case of Anna O." "Anna" was a twenty-one-year-old girl who began to manifest a wide variety of symptoms at the time of her father's final illness. These symptoms included paralysis, serious problems with both hearing and eyesight, inability to eat, ability to speak only foreign languages, a serious nervous cough, and two different alternating personalities. Working with her intensely over a year and a half, partly using hypnosis, Breuer discovered that if Anna, when in her more normal state, discussed the symptoms, she experienced some relief, and when she was able to tell of the circumstances under which a symptom began, that symptom was removed. Anna came to call this procedure "the talking cure" (Jones 1963, 142–43).

Breuer was quite engrossed in the case and was evidently slow in realizing that his wife had become unhappy because of developing jealousy. When he realized this he decided to end the treatment. Anna was in any case much better, but on the evening of the day on which he informed her of the end of the treatment he was called back only to find her suffering the pains of childbirth, though she was not in fact pregnant. It became evident that this phantom pregnancy was a hidden psychic response to Breuer's attention. Breuer brought her relief by hypnotism, and the next day he and his wife left on a trip to Venice. The girl's "imagining" of sexual involvement with him was apparently quite frightening to Breuer (ibid.). Breuer told Freud of the case of Anna O. several months after its abrupt termination. Freud was most interested, and they discussed it several times at length. In view of the understanding of hysteria that dominated the medical world at that time, the method of therapy developed by Breuer and Anna and the relative success were most remarkable. According to Ernest Jones, Freud's associate and "official" biographer, "hysteria was regarded either as a matter of simulation and at best 'imagination' (which seemed to mean much the same), on which no reputable physician would waste his time, or else a peculiar disorder of the womb which could be treated, and sometimes was treated, by extirpation of the clitoris; the wandering womb could also be driven back into its place by valerian, the smell of which it disliked" (ibid., 145).

This case did not by itself lead Freud to any startling new conclusions about hysteria, but his work with Jean Charcot in Paris some three years later did. Charcot was then the world's most renowned neurologist, and he, too, was particularly interested in hysteria. He made a careful study of hysteria using hypnosis as one of his tools. He also used his excellent knowledge of human anatomy and the "nervous system," discovering many instances in which physical disabilities were present without the physical damage that had been presumed to be the cause. That is, for example, a "paralyzed" arm or leg turned out to be entirely without the injury that would be necessary to explain the paralysis physically. He had also found hysteria in males (it being at that time a widely held medical conviction that hysteria was strictly a female malady), and he had demonstrated that its symptoms could be exactly induced in some persons by means of hypnosis.

The decisive factor here was not the use of hypnosis or the discovery of male hysteria. It was the conclusion that bodily symptoms could originate from and be treated in terms of psychic factors that are far more subtle and more powerful than malingering or imagination, indeed psychic factors of which the patient is not aware.

The development of Freud's own theories and methods came about primarily through his experience with patients. At first he employed the conventional practices of electrotherapy (not the same as present-day electric shock therapy) and hypnosis, but he became increasingly dissatisfied with both and gave them up, judging that they really impeded genuine cure.

Some of Freud's most important discoveries came in "the case of Fraulein Elisabeth von R." (begun in 1892). Since she was not responsive to hypnosis, Freud devised a new technique. He remembered a suggestion of the neurologist H. Bernheim that the apparent inability of patients to recall what had occurred during hypnosis would be overcome if the physician were sufficiently insistent that the patient could recall the experience. Freud saw that this might also be true of forgotten memories that were important in cases of hysteria (ibid., 154). To press Fraulein Elisabeth to concentrate on the forgotten memories, he had her lie down with eyes closed and instructed her to concentrate on a particular symptom in an effort to discover any memories that might bear upon its origin. He also applied pressure to her forehead with his hand when no memories were forthcoming. Sometimes after several attempts the patient would relate something that had occurred and then state that she had seen this but that she had not thought that that was what he wanted. Freud saw that he needed to add the instruction that she should try to overcome all tendencies to "censor" her thoughts, whether because she thought them unimportant or because they were unpleasant, and simply to express whatever occurred to her. This was the beginning of Freud's method of free association (ibid.).

In this first attempt to get at the origins of the symptoms in spite of the failure of hypnotism, Freud would continually question and urge the patient. But one day Frl. Elisabeth objected strongly that he was interrupting the flow of her thoughts, and Freud realized that she was right in this and that his role must be a far more quiet and patient one of trusting the process of free association.

Jones speaks of the free-association method as "a most decisive step in Freud's scientific life, the one from which all his discoveries emanated . . ." (ibid., 155–56), and argues that in the gradual process of its development several factors were at work. First among these was a firm belief in causality and determinism that Freud had learned in his medical training. Because of this conviction Freud did not assume that the seemingly meaningless wanderings of thought that the patient reported were really without significance. Instead, he judged that something must be guiding these thoughts. He believed that he found confirmation of this judgment when sooner or later a particular thought or memory would appear that provided insight into the hidden connectedness of the apparently rambling thought train (ibid., 156).

Another factor was what Freud called "resistance." He had observed that patients were consistently reluctant to tell of memories that were unpleasant. He also found, however, that if he patiently followed with them their apparently meaningless thought sequences, the significant memory would gradually be indicated (ibid.). One of his simpler illustrations is as follows:

> A stranger once invited me to drink some Italian wine with him, and in the inn he found he had forgotten the name of the wine which he had meant to order on account of his very pleasant recollections of it. A number of dissimilar substitute names occurred to him, and from these I was able to infer that the thought of someone called Hedwig had made him forget the name of the wine. Sure enough, not only did he tell me that there had been a Hedwig with him on the occasion when he first tasted the wine, but this discovery brought back to him the name he wanted. He was happily married, and "Hedwig" belonged to earlier days which he did not care to recall. (Freud 1949, 100–101)

By the use of the method of free association Freud made several important discoveries. First among these was that the memories evoked in the search for understanding of the symptoms did not stop when they reached the starting point of the symptom nor with the "traumatic" events sometimes associated with the inception of the symptoms, but they continued going back all the way to childhood (Jones 1963, 157). In other words, although an event such as an accident or the death of a loved one might be shown to have been the occasion on which the neurotic symptoms appeared, such traumatic events only had this effect of producing neurotic symptoms when they were somehow deeply related to a susceptibility in a hidden emotional structure that had developed much earlier in the life of a patient.

The method of free association also led to the conclusion that dreams have meaning and that their meaning is of the utmost importance for the under-standing of human beings. This discovery arose from the fact that when pa-tients talked of their symptoms in searching for their origins, they also talked of their dreams. The continuing process of free association would eventually bring to light the inner connection of the dream symbolisms with the other thoughts and the symptoms. Thus dreams were found to provide valuable clues to the origins of the neuroses.

It was Freud's conviction that every element of a dream is significant. One of his examples was from a long dream of one of his patients in which the pa-tient dreamed of several members of his family being seated at a table of a special shape. In relating the associations that this dream element suggested, the dreamer recalled that a family he had visited had such a table. Then he noted that the relation between father and son in that family was peculiar, and, finally, that his relations to his father were of the same nature. The in-terpretation that the table was employed in the dream in order to show this similarity was supported by the discovery that the name of the family the pa-tient had visited and then dreamt of was "Tischler," *Tisch* being the German word for "table" (Freud 1949, 107–8).

Freud's very extensive study of dreams together with his other discoveries by means of the free-association method led him to the conclusion that just as traumas are not sufficient to produce the neurotic symptoms unless there is a "predisposition" rooting back in childhood experience, so also the present events that contribute the manifest forms of the dream are not sufficient to account for the dream apart from the dynamic role of unconscious factors rooted in childhood or even in infantile experience.

A more startling discovery was that sexual factors regularly play a major role in our dreams. The well-known emphasis Freud placed upon sexuality and his claim that even infants have a rich sexual life were probably the greatest source of opposition to his teachings. It was the data arising from the free-association method and from dream interpretation that played the cen-tral role in leading Freud to the judgment that sexuality is so important. It was not a conclusion for which he looked or which he liked. Rather, it was, in his judgment, simply a matter of fact as indicated by the data.

Among the unexpected and unpleasant data produced by patients with quite surprising frequency were reports of sexual assault by an adult when they (the patients) were children, and more often than not the guilty party was the father. Freud became convinced that such events must be quite common, and continued for several years to hold the conventional view that young children are utterly devoid of sexual impulse and interest. It was only by the aid of his own painstaking self-analysis that he came to recognize that these reports of incestuous assaults on children were not factually true and that small children are not without sexuality. To his amazement he discovered that he himself had as a child been sexually interested in his mother and jealous of his father. He recognized the reports of assaults by adults on children to be the result of fantasies produced by the childhood sexual interests (Jones 1963, 205–9).

Freud's doctrine of infantile sexuality seems less improbable when the breadth of his concept is recognized. It has been common to think of sexual experience in terms of the genitals, but it is not so restricted for Freud. In his view the first two stages of the development of human sexuality are the *oral* and the *anal* stages. The former is that period associated with the first year of life when pleasure is obtained primarily by way of the mouth. The latter Freud saw primarily in ages one to three, during which time he found that pleasure is derived from the retention and expulsion of feces. He also found this period to be one in which one's interests are primarily focused upon oneself and in which satisfaction is found primarily in terms of one's own body.

One might ask why such infantile sources of pleasure should be called "sexual." The answer lay in Freud's conviction that these pleasure foci were but developmental stages toward normal adult sexuality and in his discovery, as he believed, that the difficulties of patients were entangled with their not having genuinely progressed out of these early developmental stages.

A unifying concept may be found in Freud's doctrine of "libido." This term designates the psychic energy of the life force which motivates a person's drives. Freud concluded that it is basically a striving for pleasure, and that because the most intense pleasure is in sexual relations, the libidinal energy is primarily sexual.

Dr. A. A. Brill explains the concept as follows:

> In psychoanalysis libido signifies that quantitatively changeable and not at present measurable energy of the sexual instinct which is usually directed to an outside object. It comprises all those impulses which deal with love in the broad sense. Its main component is sexual love; and sexual union is the aim; but it also includes self-love, love for parents and children, friendship, attachments to concrete objects, and even devotion to abstract ideas. (Freud 1938, 16)

The focus, then, of this energy orally or anally in an infant is part of the "sexual" life of the developing person. Those stages are ordinarily succeeded about age three by the "phallic" stage in which the libido focuses upon the penis or the clitoris, and this stage is then followed shortly by the Oedipal stage, about ages three to seven. Freud believed that in this period it is usual to develop sexual interest toward the parent of the opposite sex and a desire to take the place of the parent of the same sex.

Frustration of the libido, the principal driving force of one's life, is not only possible but likely at any and all of these stages. The "pleasure principle," that persons are basically motivated by the desire for pleasure, comes into conflict with the "reality principle," for reality commonly does not allow an unimpeded pursuit of pleasure. The gratification the infant seeks by way of the mouth is not always available when wanted. The anal pleasures may well conflict with the parental wishes, evoking hostility. Parents have commonly interfered with the small child's enjoyment of his or her own genitals, and the Oedipal period is inevitably one of frustration, for the child cannot wholly displace the parent of the same sex. This frustration sometimes results in "repression" of the denied desire and leads to neurotic symptoms.

The concept of repression, like Freud's other concepts, was derived from observations in his work with patients (and from his own self-analysis). One of the surprising discoveries was that the patients who had come for help nevertheless resisted it. As Freud wrote in 1915, "when we undertake to cure a patient of his symptoms he opposes against us a vigorous and tenacious *resistance* throughout the entire course of the treatments" (Freud 1949, 253). Long and careful observation of these resistances showed them to be powerful, subtle, ingenious, and quite varied. It also revealed that they were strongest when the process of the analysis was close to making conscious to the patient something about him or her that was painful or objectionable, but that after it had been consciously acknowledged by the patient the resistance was gone.

These studies led to two conclusions: (1) that there are powerful forces at work opposing the sought-after change in the neurotic condition, and (2) that these must be the same forces that produced the condition (ibid., 258–59). Freud argued that the existence of the neurotic symptom showed

> that some mental process had not been carried through to an end in a normal manner so that it could become conscious; the symptom is a substitute for that which has not come through. . . . A vehement effort must have been exercised to prevent the mental process in question from penetrating into consciousness and as a result it has remained unconscious; being unconscious it had the power to construct a symptom. (Ibid., 259)

Freud was concerned with distinguishing this process of repression-producing symptoms from the familiar conscious process of rejecting one's own thoughts and impulses. He believed that when one does this consciously the psychic energy involved in the impulse is withdrawn. One may well remember the impulse, but insofar as the process at work is entirely conscious, the impulse has become powerless. By contrast, repression is a process of which the conscious self is quite unaware. There is no memory of the event, but the impulse retains its energy (ibid.).

It is thus repression that accounts for "the Unconscious" in Freud's earlier view. The unconscious does not simply designate things of which one happens not to be conscious. Its "contents" are dynamic, alive, possess energy, are beyond the reach and powers of the conscious self, and have power over the conscious self. This power is manifest in dreams (wherein that which is repressed is able to come to expression only in "censored" form so that consciousness remains protected from that which it does not wish to acknowledge about itself), in neurotic symptoms, and in the resistance to discovery of that which is repressed.

One might infer from this brief description that in Freud's theory only the ill have repressions and therefore an unconscious. This would, however, be far from his belief—except in the sense in which he was willing to say that all persons are neurotic in some degree. Freud devoted extensive studies to showing that the unconscious is an important factor in the daily lives of "normal," "healthy" people. In his *Psychopathology of Everyday Life* he sought at length to show that the forgetting of proper names and foreign words, slips of the tongue, and various kinds of common errors are not meaningless accidents but are significant clues to the life of the unconscious in all of us. In other writings he went on to interpret virtually every aspect of life and culture in terms of his conviction that the unconscious is the primary factor in human life.

During many years of continuing study, therapeutic practice, and dialogue with other doctors and scholars, Freud developed a more complex understanding of the unconscious and of the human psyche as a whole. A full statement appeared in *The Ego and the Id*, which was first published in 1923. Here the term "id" (or "it") represents the original, chaotic state of the undeveloped mentality in the child (and in the earlier state of the species). Through contact with the external world (by way of perception) the ego (or "I") develops. That is, a part of the id develops as an agent of adaptation to the demands and pressures of reality. This means that the ego has the task of guiding, controlling, restricting, and resisting the impulses and drives of instinct working through the id.

The ego and the id do not simply restate the conflict of consciousness—under pressure from "the reality principle"—and the unconscious—driven by "the pleasure principle." First, the ego, which has arisen from the id, is still "rooted" therein, and it remains partly unconscious. Second, a part of that which is unconscious is distinguished as "preconscious." This term designates whatever happens to be in the psyche that is not conscious but can easily become conscious. The most obvious example would be memories that are not blocked by repression. Third, in the course of the normal development of the individual, a portion of the ego is modified into the "super-ego."

Its content is an "ego ideal" that results from the "introjection" of the father-identification and the mother-identification when the Oedipus complex is resolved. The most familiar way in which the super-ego is experienced is as "conscience," that within us which tells us what we should be and do and what we should not be and do. Though the super-ego develops as a modification of the ego, it is essentially unconscious, and it is closer to the id than the ego is. Repression is now understood to be done by the ego (though not consciously) usually in response to pressure from the super-ego. In his *New Introductory Lectures on Psychoanalysis* (1933), Freud offered a diagrammatic aid to grasping the basic relationships of this more complex understanding of the human psyche (Freud 1965, 70).

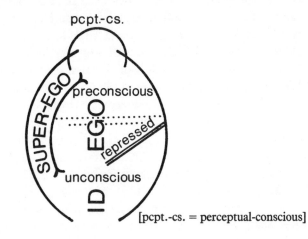

[pcpt.-cs. = perceptual-conscious]

The importance of the ego in the midst of the complexity of factors was explained by Freud:

By virtue of its relation to the perceptual system it gives mental processes an order in time and submits them to "reality testing." By interposing the processes of thinking, it secures a postponement of motor discharges and controls the access to motility. This last power is, to be sure, a question more of form than of fact; in the matter of action the ego's position is like that of a constitutional monarch, without whose sanction no law can be passed but who hesitates long before imposing his veto on any measure put forward by Parliament. All the experiences of life that originate from without enrich the ego; the id, however, is its second external world, which it strives to bring into subjection to itself. It withdraws libido from the id and transforms the object-cathexes of the id into ego-structures. With the aid of the super-ego, in a manner that is still obscure to us, it draws upon the experiences of past ages stored in the id. (Freud 1960, 74)

As this statement suggests, Freud saw the position of the ego as important but embattled, and in the same context he said,

we see this same ego as a poor creature owing service to three masters and consequently menaced by three dangers: from the external world, from the libido of the id, and from the severity of the super-ego. . . . Whenever possible, it tries to remain on good terms with the id; it clothes the id's *Ucs.* [unconscious] demands with its *Pcs.* [preconscious] rationalizations; it pretends that the id is showing obedience to the admonitions of reality, even when in fact it is remaining obstinate and unyielding; it disguises the id's conflicts with reality and, if possible, its conflicts with the super-ego too. In its position midway between the id and reality, it only too often yields to the temptation to become sycophantic, opportunist and lying, like a politician who sees the truth but wants to keep his place in popular favor. (Ibid., 75)

Nevertheless, the hope for human health and peace lies, in Freud's view, in the conquest—insofar as possible—of the id by the ego, and it was the purpose of psychoanalysis to aid in this process.

For Freud, this hope was indeed a limited one, and though this should already be evident even from this brief summary of the complex factors pressing in upon the ego, there is yet another basic complicating factor that Freud found to be at work. In his book *Beyond the Pleasure Principle* (1920) he presented his conclusion that there is a death instinct in addition to Eros (the life-pleasure-sexual instinct). This death instinct, though not as obvious as Eros, is an ever-present natural drive to return the organism to its original state. There is thus a deep and original conflict at work in the id itself in addition to the conflicts of the pleasure principle with the reality principle, of consciousness with repressions, and of the ego with the super-ego. The human psyche is a battleground with the ego caught in the middle, and evidently, for Freud, its only real peace comes with the eventual victory of the death instinct.

Freud's theories were considerably more complex than these summaries indicate, and they were also in a continuing process of change and development. One of the influences on these developments was dialogue and disagreement with those who were deeply impressed by Freud's work. It was inevitable that criticisms and alternatives would be offered by some of these persons.

The first major alternative was proposed by Alfred Adler (1870–1937). Adler worked very closely with Freud from 1902 until 1911, though it appears that they never really agreed on the basic character of the human psyche. Adler began his research as a physician with a special interest in organ inferiorities. His studies led him from this biological focus to a psychological emphasis in which he judged that the human being is motivated primarily by feelings of inferiority. This root motivation of human life was inevitable, he concluded, because of both the origins of the human species in the evolutionary process and the beginnings of each individual human life. The developments that enabled the survival of our predecessors and the emergence of our species were impelled by inferiority to creatures that were in many ways better equipped for the battle. The human psyche was produced, argued Adler, by the need for greater intelligence in order to overcome creatures that were naturally better protected. Hence inferiority is the deepest root and impetus of psychic energy. This is then reinforced by the helplessness of human infants and the unusually long period of childhood dependence as compared to other creatures.

Adler did not see this judgment as a negative one, for in his view these inferiority feelings were the motivating force for human sociality, culture, science, and every real human advance. Social feeling is therefore also a characteristic deeply rooted in human origins. It requires development, however, and Adler came to see it as the essential basis for distinguishing the normal from the abnormal personality.

On such bases Adler came to reject as reductionistic the Freudian view of the unconscious as constituted by repression and of psychic energy as primarily sexual. He also rejected the therapeutic approach of searching back into childhood and infancy, for he believed such data as symptoms and dreams to show that the psyche is striving toward an overcoming of inferiority. The need, therefore, is to discern the aim of the psyche rather than its history. Adler also repudiated the division of the psyche into conscious and unconscious "parts," so it could be questioned whether his was a depth psychology. Nevertheless, his own emphasis upon the fundamental role of deeply hidden inferiority feelings and the motivation of persons by an unconsciously developed life's goal and style of life—together oriented toward overcoming the inferiority feelings—show him to have shared with Freud the conviction that unconscious psychic factors are of primary importance in human thought, feeling, and motivation.

Adler's teachings, which are barely suggested here, continue to be very influential, but they do not differ as profoundly from Freud's as do those of another early collaborator, C. G. Jung.

CARL GUSTAV JUNG

Carl Gustav Jung (1875–1961), a third great pioneer in depth psychology, argued that these contrasting theories of Freud and Adler could both be included within a broader and deeper understanding of the unconscious. He agreed with Adler that Freud's interpretation of the unconscious in terms of repressed infantile sexual wishes was reductionistic, but he did not agree that such factors are to be entirely cast aside or that they are simply to be replaced by a reinterpretation of psychic energy as striving to overcome inferiorities. Adler's view, he held, is also reductionistic. Psychic energy does not just move forward rather than backward. It moves both ways, and it also moves inward and outward. These movements of psychic energy are not the same in all persons, however, but differ in rather basic ways. So Jung developed a theory of psychological types as a way of interpreting these differences. In this sense his understanding of the unconscious is broader than either Freud's or Adler's.

More important, Jung's theories offer a "deeper" understanding of the unconscious, for he became convinced that there is another "layer" of the unconscious beyond the personal factors considered by Freud and Adler. Jung called this the "collective unconscious."

In the course of years of work as a psychiatrist, Jung repeatedly encountered symbolic patterns and themes in the dreams, fantasies, visions, and delusions of his patients that he found could not be adequately accounted for on the basis of the personal experience of the individuals reporting them. He also found that the symptoms and disturbances that were somehow entangled with these symbolisms were not resolvable as long as they were treated simply in terms of the supposition that they arose entirely from personal experience. He came to the realization that these symbolic themes were essentially like those that have appeared in the mythologies, rituals, and art of all the earlier cultures for which we have the appropriate data.

One would assume that the persons having the dreams and symptoms had learned of these symbolic patterns through language and education. Jung was particularly struck, however, by instances in which that possibility was ruled out, because, for example, the particular ancient mythic theme was completely unknown, or the dreams were those of young children (Jung 1964, 69).

On the basis of extensive study of these phenomena Jung came to the conclusion that in addition to the personal factors—both conscious and unconscious—in the human psyche, "there exists a second psychic system of a collective, universal, and impersonal nature which is identical in all individuals. This collective unconscious does not develop individually but is inherited. It consists of pre-existent forms, the archetypes, which can only become conscious secondarily and which give definite form to certain psychic contents" (Jung 1968a, 43). All of this is understood to have developed over the course of millions of years of evolution of human beings, prior to and during the struggle for the development of consciousness.

This hypothesis of a "collective unconsciousness" has been rejected by most psychologists and has frequently been spoken of scornfully. To others, however, it has seemed strange that we can so readily believe in remarkable inheritances among other creatures, such as the abilities of birds to build complex nests, care for their young, and make the same long annual journeys guided by inherited instincts, but still suppose by contrast that the human psyche inherits nothing—that every human is born with an empty "mind."

Jung did an enormous amount of research into Eastern, African, and American Indian religions and myths, and into Gnosticism, alchemy, astrology, art, and ritual in the "West," until he became convinced—*as a scientist*—by a vast amount of data that there is indeed in every human being an "archaic inheritance" of great symbolic power.

This conclusion was not, for Jung, merely a matter of academic interest. He was persuaded that the long struggle of our ancestors to gain consciousness and the further struggle to develop conscious reason and use it to understand and subdue nature by the thinking and the science that are our most powerful instruments have cut us off from natural dimensions of our own potential wholeness and thus from the nature that is our "mother" and our home. We think we dominate nature, but our individual and collective lives belie this pride. It seems clear that we do not control our motives and feelings. We are evidently unable to reason together to find peace, feed the hungry, and stop the abuse and exploitation of both persons and the environment. It may be that nature still dominates us.

Jung had no desire to repudiate reason and science. He wished, rather, to use them to discern their limits and find their potential. Late in his career he wrote, "Modern man does not understand how much his 'rationalism' (which has destroyed his capacity to respond to numinous symbols and ideas) has put him at the mercy of the psychic 'underworld'" (Jung 1964, 94).

Nevertheless, we can, he believed, learn to "listen" to and cooperate with our own psychic depths and gain thereby greater wholeness and freedom. It is the archetypal dream symbolisms that compensate for our alienation from nature and from which, therefore, we can learn more of ourselves so that we may become more of what we are capable of being.

Something of the nature of the understanding of the human psyche that Jung developed may be suggested by the following diagram. It should be recognized, however, that no attempt is made herein to depict the relative power or importance of the three "layers" of the psyche. First of all, that is not known. The Unconscious is unknown and unknowable. Its reality and its workings can only be inferred from various indications that are themselves in the realm of consciousness. Further, Jung emphatically rejected the charge that he valued the unconscious more highly than consciousness, and he frequently warned against any surrender of the achievements, the values, and the judgments of the latter. It should also be understood that the horizontal lines in the diagram that distinguish the three "layers" should not be taken to suggest that there are clear and distinct lines of separation. Insofar as consciousness can see, these dimensions of the psyche "shade into" each other or overlap.

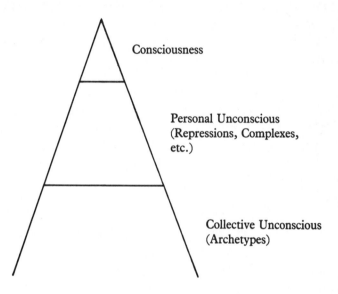

No line is drawn at the bottom of the diagram, because the "depths" of the unconscious are unknowable, and the deeper psyche is to be understood as rooted in nature (Jung 1968b, 24).

The "contents" of the collective unconscious are—in Jung's developed theory—called *archetypes*. An earlier designation, "primordial images," had led too easily to the misunderstanding that Jung meant something specific and imaginable. Quite the contrary, the term "archetypes" refers to unknowable potentialities or propensities for mythic and symbolic representations associated with strong "feeling-toned" experiences. The existence of such archetypes was inferred from the observation of similar symbolic patterns and themes in the myths of many cultures, the rituals of the various religions, the dreams of countless persons, and many such phenomena.

Another clue to the collective unconscious and its archetypes was seen in certain cases of "projection." Projection, as Freud taught, is a situation in which something in the psyche of a person is "seen" or experienced by that person as being in someone or something else. It is the unconscious that "projects." Thus, for example, one may (unconsciously) project a parental imago (the emotionally powerful unconscious image of one's father or mother) upon another person. One will then react under certain circumstances to that other person in accordance with the repressed relationship to the parent rather than in appropriate response to that person. Freud, Jung, and other therapists found that when one gained insight into one's projecting, the projection would sometimes be withdrawn with a resulting increase in ego-strength and a better relationship.

In studying the cases in which this withdrawal of the projection of the parental imagos did not follow the recognition (as shown by the continuation of the symptoms of disturbance), Jung concluded that in such cases something "deeper" and more meaningful than a parental imago was being projected, namely, one's own contrasexual psychic aspect. For in every man there is a feminine aspect and in every woman a masculine aspect manifested in countless expressions of an archetype of the collective unconscious. He called this aspect in a man the *anima*, and in a woman the *animus*.

If a man has not accepted his feminine side, it will be projected, ordinarily upon a woman or women whose characteristics facilitate such projection. Since a man's anima may have taken on some of its more particular characteristics from his mother (its deeper nature being, however, born with his psyche) it is not surprising to find it projected sometimes upon a woman or women who in some ways resemble the mother. But the power of the relationship is stronger than that which comes only from the projection of the mother imago, for in the case of projection of the anima, it is the unrecognized and unacknowledged "other side" of one's self that one is relating to. In these circumstances the anima may represent the deeper unconscious as well as the contrasexual side of the man's psyche. Such a man is, therefore, alienated from himself, and the attempt to gain wholeness through the other person will fail unless the insight and the withdrawal of the projection occur. Because that which is projected is deeper and more powerful than mere projection of the parental imago, such a resolution is both more difficult and more important (Jung 1968a, 65–67).

In Jung's judgment, it is not only that these archetypes of the masculine and the feminine are deeper and more powerful than factors in the personal unconscious such as the parental imagos, but the archetypes are present in the child's psyche *first*, from the beginning, so the literal parents are initially experienced in terms of these archetypes. To deal only with factors in the personal unconscious, as in Freudian theory, is therefore superficial.

Another illustration of the difference between the two depth psychologies can be seen in the interpretation of dreams that manifest the theme of incest.

For the Freudian such dreams are understood—generally—to reveal the Oedipus situation, the desire to possess sexually the parent of the opposite sex. For Jung, however, even though he did not deny that sometimes a person may have such unconscious incestuous desires and that dreams may point to this, in cases of strong feeling-toned dreams the presence of archetypal expression is to be suspected, and the incest motif—as suggested also by its mythological representations—is judged to be indicative of a desire for the restoration of wholeness (Jung 1966, 218, etc.).

The central archetype of the psyche's drive toward wholeness is the archetype of the *Self*. The general assumption in "Western" cultures is that "self" and "ego" are one and the same, both designating whatever one means in saying "I." This usually indicates one's *conscious* centeredness, and consciousness is assumed to be the very essence of the healthy person. The depth psychologies of Freud and Adler largely share this judgment. Although they emphasized the roles of unconscious factors, they sought ways to reduce or eliminate them, leaving the conscious "I" in command of the personality.

Jung judged the data he studied to show the potential wholeness of a person to be much greater than the ego can ever become and to require a cooperation between the conscious self and its unconscious dimensions. He agreed that the complexes of the personal unconscious should be divested of their pathological power by insight, but in his view this was not to put the ego in charge. Rather it opened the way for dealing constructively with the collective unconscious.

The "Self" in Jungian terminology refers to an archetype, a dynamic nucleus or core of the potential wholeness of a person expressed in a great variety of mythical figures and dream symbolisms. Effective encounter with these is commonly prevented by failure to gain insight into one's repressions and complexes, by not accepting the presence in one's psyche of motivations that are contrary to one's conscious values (not "realizing the Shadow"), and by the refusal to accept one's contrasexual side (anima/animus). However, as M.-L. von Franz has put it,

> if an individual has wrestled seriously enough and long enough with the anima (or animus) problem so that he, or she, is no longer partially identified with it, the unconscious again changes its dominant character and appears in a new symbolic form, representing the Self, the innermost nucleus of the psyche. In dreams of a woman this center is usually personified as a superior female figure—a priestess, sorceress, earth mother, or goddess of nature or love. In the case of a man, it manifests itself as a masculine initiator and guardian (an Indian *guru*), a wise old man, a spirit of nature, and so forth. (Jung 1964, 196)

The question hereby raised for the ego is whether it will risk cooperating with the Self, or, more generally, whether consciousness will accept aid from the unconscious psyche. The ego is tempted to try to shut out or to dominate the Self, for it fears being swallowed up by the Self, and that sometimes happens. But if the potential wholeness of the person is to be more fully achieved, the ego must give up the desire to maintain complete control and risk this dialogue. When this is done a person gains great psychic strength and continues to grow toward greater wholeness (Jung 1969, 224).

Jung made a further point about the archetype of the Self that has been particularly disturbing to some. In his judgment one cannot clearly distinguish that archetype from the image of God. "The self . . . is a God-image, or at least cannot be distinguished from one" (Jung 1968b, 22). "The symbols of the self coincide with those of the Deity. The self is not the ego, it symbolizes the totality of man and he is obviously not whole without God" (Jung 1955, 719). Some see in this an importing of religion into science, while others take it to be a reduction of the religious to the merely psychological. Jung was scrupulous in his efforts to avoid both of these confusions. He was usually explicit about speaking as a scientist and describing data while recognizing the inability of science to make metaphysical judgments. Religious experience is a fact of humankind, and in Jung's judgment it is essential to human health. The affirmation of the reality of God beyond the phenomena of human experience is a matter of *belief*, he insisted, and he tried to keep his own metaphysical or religious beliefs and convictions out of his scientific work. That he believed in God seems to be clear enough from his more personal statements (see his autobiographical *Memories, Dreams, Reflections*), provided one does not require some orthodox definition of "God." Jung's personal beliefs are not, however, of concern here.

These brief sketches can hardly be expected to convey a clear understanding of Jungian depth psychology, but they may suffice to suggest the contrast of Jung's understanding of human beings with those of Freud and Adler. The basic difference is in Jung's affirmation of the collective unconscious. This entails further contrasts. The unconscious is essentially negative for Freud, an impediment to health. For both Freud and Adler the unconscious is, insofar as possible, to be removed so that conscious reasoning may control the person. For Jung the unconscious is essentially positive, for though it is a source of threat and disturbance for the person, it is also a profound source of strength and enrichment and therefore to be cooperated with.

These very substantial disagreements should not, however, be allowed to obscure the basic general agreement among the depth psychologists. For although they differ on the question of *how* the unconscious psychic factors in persons should be understood, they agree *that* human beings must be understood in terms of such unconscious depths. In the powerful ways in which they set forth and tested this conclusion, Freud, Adler, Jung, and their colleagues pioneered a profoundly important revolution in modern human self-interpretation that has affected the understanding of every dimension of human being and doing.

THE SIGNIFICANCE OF DEPTH PSYCHOLOGY FOR CHRISTIAN THEOLOGY

In offering a substantial reinterpretation of the nature of human beings, depth psychologies of whatever variety call for a reconsideration of every aspect of the theological enterprise. Theology is *not* simply "the science of God," for as a would-be "science," even in the general sense of a disciplined search for knowledge, theology is a human enterprise carried on in human words, concepts, and figures of speech. It is practiced by humans and for humans seeking understanding of the vexing complexities of human existence and meaning in and for human life and destiny. Every aspect of method and every doctrine must be reconsidered *if* it is judged that there are indeed powerful unconscious depths in the human psyche.

We are not concerned here with the personal religious convictions of the psychologists. Freud and Jung both had much to say about religion and religious phenomena. Freud reached deeply negative conclusions about religious beliefs, but his basic understanding of the human psyche did not require these conclusions, and many theoreticians and therapists who may be described as Freudian or neo-Freudian have disagreed with Freud on this subject. Similarly, although Jung took an essentially positive view of religion, he was well aware that his researches as a psychologist did not justify any judgment as to the transcendent truth or untruth of religious convictions, and Jungians have sometimes disagreed with him on this whole subject.

Christian theology begins with faith commitment and seeks to understand how this faith came to be and what it means. In this enterprise all theologians are influenced by their convictions and/or assumptions concerning human nature. Those who suppose that these simply come from Scripture or revelation are manifestly naive or self-deceived. Most serious theologians therefore devote careful attention to questions about human nature and critically study the judgments and findings of nontheological specialists—including psychologists—in search of assistance. Both Freud and Jung have been influential among some theologians, and their influence is growing. But it remains the theologians' responsibility to examine such teachings critically in light of what are judged to be appropriate criteria. In this process, it is not the personal religious convictions of the psychologists but their findings about human beings that are of potential importance to the work of the theologians.

Although there are some general points of common relevance for theology in all depth psychologies, it is more helpful to consider separately the views of Jung (with his affirmation of the collective unconscious) and other views such as those of Freud and Adler (who see the unconscious essentially as an unfortunate appendage to consciousness limited to what Jung called the personal unconscious).

In the case of these latter views it is easier for the theologian to suppose that the work of theology per se need not be affected by the recognition of the unconscious, for one might judge that it is the responsibility of the therapists to set free those whose minds are clouded by unconscious factors, while the work of the theologians is to be carried on by and for persons who do not share those infringements upon rationality. Freud and his followers would offer warnings, however, to those who take the unconscious so lightly. Freud became convinced not only that the power of the unconscious is to be found in all persons—not just in the "pathological"—but that unconscious factors cannot fully be removed. Adler was rather more optimistic about the possibilities of gaining freedom from unconscious influences, but he shared the judgment concerning their universality and hardly regarded their conquest as either simple or common.

Both of these depth psychologies require a rethinking of the more familiar understandings of the human problem expressed in traditional Christian views of "sin." Often these beliefs have assumed that human beings, from the beginning, have been morally free and simply guilty of willful disobedience to the will of God and therefore deserving of punishment. Such assumptions are familiar enough today. They provide the central motifs for many understandings of the drama of salvation, indeed of the whole theological edifice. And these theologies carry with them ethical teachings that entail the same presuppositions regarding human freedom and responsibility. The usual qualification is that those who "accept Jesus Christ" are now the only ones who are truly free to fulfill God's will, but they at least are expected by exercise of their will power to act always in a Christlike manner, being subject to condemnation for failures to do so.

If any depth-psychological understanding of human motivations is taken seriously, the foregoing interpretation of "sin" must be rejected as false and destructive. Consider, for example, the common interpretation of one of the Ten Commandments according to which children are taught that they are under sacred obligation to love their parents, and the interpretation of a portion of the Sermon on the Mount as a moral imperative that condemns anger toward another person. They are taken together here, for, understood depth psychologically, they become entangled in human experience.

A human child is born into a state of utter helplessness and dependency. She is dependent upon her parents or parental surrogates not only for food, shelter, etc., but also for the recognition, affection, affirmation, love upon which her ability to realize that she is someone and that she is of value are built. The parents are "gods" to the infant and the small child. But all parents are complex and limited creatures. They are not always present, do not always understand, are sometimes quite preoccupied with other concerns even when dealing with the child's physical needs. To a greater or lesser degree each parent is subject to anxiety, impatience, frustration, and anger. Hence to varying degrees an infant will experience a lack of affirmation and love. It has long been known that a human infant all of whose physical needs are provided but who is denied all direct human contact will usually die. That is but one indication of how fundamental is the need for human attention and most basically for love. To the greater degree that the infant does not experience this acceptance and affirmation from these parental "gods," the infant will be less able to develop a sense of being acceptable and be susceptible to a deep sense of unworthiness. The infant and small child will also experience frustration which leads to anger. But anger at the "gods" is felt to be self-destructive. It is terrifying. It also produces guilt feelings that serve as evidence of the unworthiness. This process is commonly reinforced by the parental responses (of various sorts) to the child's anger. This too is frustrating, and a vicious circle of frustration > anger > guilt > frustration easily ensues. All of this is overwhelming, so the unconscious aids the child by repressing these feelings and memories.

From various depth-psychological points of view, this is—roughly—the usual situation in varying degrees. These repressions do not constitute the only feelings and motivations in the growing child, but they constitute an aspect of *ambivalence*, the common state of human feelings of mixed or conflicting elements. The repressions, by definition unknown to the one whose repressions they are (and not usually recognized by others either), are a dynamic reality within the psyche that can emerge or even "erupt" under various stimuli. Much family strife is so motivated, and not just by the repressions of the children, for one may expect them to be at work in all members of the family. Further, the repressed anger is often "spilled" on persons other than the one or ones toward whom the anger was originally felt, most powerfully in situations involving projection.

It is not difficult to see that the demands to love parents and never to feel anger toward a "brother," imposed as laws of God with the assumption that persons are ordinarily simply able to decide to have the one emotion and to avoid the other, are utterly unrealistic. They also aggravate the psychic tension already present—with varying results for differing persons—and reinforce the deep confusion of God with the unconscious parental imagos. Among common results are unconscious fear of and anger with God. It is not difficult to see why so many therapists have judged that religion is a major source of pathology, dehumanization, and destruction.

It should be equally evident that it will not help—from a depth-psychological point of view—to demand of Christians who insist upon legalistic, moralistic, judgmental, and retributive interpretations of their religion that they surrender those interpretations in light of the foregoing reasoning, for those religious orientations are themselves—usually—maintained for unconscious "reasons" such as the need to project rather than acknowledge some of one's own feelings and motivations, the need to find some sense of affirmation by identifying those others as the "bad ones" condemned by the God to whom one believes him- or herself to be "faithful," and so forth. All such unconscious motivations are, of course, also strong sources of resistance to recognition of unconscious motivating factors!

Another graphic illustration of the importance to the theologians of the questions raised by Freudian and neo-Freudian depth psychology may be seen in Anna Marie Rizzuto's *The Birth of the Living God*. It is a report and interpretation of clinical research on the origin, development, and significance of persons' God representations. The author, a clinical professor of psychiatry, carefully studied data from questionnaires, drawings, case histories, intensive and extensive interviews, etc., to learn of the largely unconscious God representations of twenty persons, and of the relationships of these God representations to the growth and development, adjustments or maladjustments, and religious beliefs in each of these persons' lives. The study included both patients in therapy and regular members of the staff at the hospital where the research was conducted. On the basis of the general conclusions reached, no significant differences were found between the patients and the staff members. She also studied a vast array of potentially relevant published material.

Among the conclusions reached in this process are: (1) God representations that are powerful psychic realities develop before concepts of God. (2) The small child's experience of the parents is usually the most significant factor in the formation of these representations, sometimes the father being most influential and sometimes the mother, though other relationships also contribute. (3) There is a powerful interrelationship of the God representation and the self representation of a person. (4) There is a need for re-creation of the

God representation at each developmental crisis in one's life if there is to be a healthy relevance of beliefs in a person's psyche. (5) There is a correlation of arrested development in the personality and in the God representation, and this may occur at any stage in the developmental process. (6) A person's *beliefs* regarding the reality of God and a person's *concepts* of God may be profoundly in conflict with that person's *God representations*. (7) The greater power in such cases is—by far—in the God representations, not in the concepts nor even in the conscious *denial* of the reality of God. (8) In instances of such conflicts (often aggravated by "official" religious teachings) there is great potential for emotional strife within individuals, among family members, and in other important relationships.

To this partial list should be added a point of disagreement with some of the teachings of Freud, for Dr. Rizzuto who starts with Freud and is generally persuaded of the soundness of his perspective nevertheless concludes that the side of Freud's teaching which sought to dispose of religious "illusions" was wrong. Her study persuaded her that God representations are ineradicable and indispensable. Hence, "The Freud who *believes* that man lives on the bread of knowledge alone, I have to disagree with." Yet she agrees with "the other Freud," the one who wrote, "The idea of a single great god—an idea which must be recognized as a completely justified memory, . . . has a compulsive character: it *must* be believed . . ." (Rizzuto 1979, 212).

If one will ponder such clinical findings, one will readily see that much of the strategy of theologians, preachers, religious educators, and others in religious roles (not the least, parents) is based upon naively oversimplified assumptions about human motivations, capacities to learn and to change, and moral freedom. Among other things, the often supposed importance of doctrinal correctness ("orthodoxy") is called into question, and it is implied (at least) that symbolic meanings seen in relationship to the becoming or nonbecoming of persons are—as a matter of fact—far more important. One may also see a possible answer to the question of why it is that religion is both so creative and so destructive a dimension of human life. Theology, in turn, can be seen to be in danger of irrelevance or even of destructiveness if carried on in ignorance of such human dynamics as are pointed to in this study.

One might again be tempted to suppose that these points are of importance only in relationship to "pathological" personalities and therefore of concern to therapists but not to theologians. The study does not support this conclusion, however. What proportion of our society is made up of psychically "mature" persons is subject to debate, but the evidence adduced points to a complexity of motivational factors including unconscious ones bearing directly on the theological agenda *in all persons*.

To the warnings the Freudian understanding of the human psyche offers to the theologian, the Jungian will add yet more—and the Jungian will also add hopes. In the case of the data offered by studies such as those of Dr. Rizzuto, the Jungian would urge the addition of attention to archetypal factors. Dr. Rizzuto did not find these, but that is hardly surprising, for her assumptions and questions did not entertain the possibility. Jungians' observations have led them to the conclusion that these factors *must* be present, for the child experiences the mother and father in terms of archetypes first of all. They are the forms of experience with which each of us comes into the world before the personal unconscious or clarity of consciousness has developed. Under their influence, the parents are "mythologized," and the gradual distinguishing of the real parents as the child becomes increasingly conscious is an important and often painful process (Jung 1968a, 67). Further, "The God-image is not something *invented*, it is an *experience* that comes upon man spontaneously . . . ," that is, from the collective unconscious (Jung 1968b, 194). Here, as elsewhere, the archetype of the Self is seen to be working toward the wholeness of the individual. From the standpoint of faith, it is God who is experienced as at work here in the individual, though that judgment cannot be made by the psychologist as psychologist.

From a Jungian standpoint, then, the Freudian interpretation makes the mistake of reducing the dynamic factors at work in human lives and thereby blinds persons to powerful influences that might be crucial sources of help toward wholeness. If the Jungian view is the more correct understanding, the human enterprise is both more difficult and more hopeful—particularly for a culture like ours which for the most part resists such a perspective and is largely cut off from powerful symbolic meanings.

At the root of that hopefulness is the experience/conviction that holy and gracious being is at work within us offering help in our task of becoming. A lesser hope entailed herein is the realization that even if the majority of professional theologians continue to suppose that their doctrinal reformulations are correctly describing the nature and the will of the Deity, symbolic expressions of numinous meanings will nevertheless be at work among us, arising from the collective unconscious, appearing in dreams, expressed in Scriptures, in rituals and hymns, in art and literature, in myth and in nature. Interestingly enough, even when the academic theologians have supposed that theirs was the primary language of a religious community, symbolic expressions have seemed to flourish.

This contention impinges most obviously upon the issues of language and meaning in theology and affects the whole doctrinal enterprise. When one begins to consider the power of doctrines of the Trinity, the Christ, the Holy

Spirit, and the Sacraments in light of the archetypes of the collective unconscious, a whole new dimension of meaning begins to open up, and works that seek to explore these possibilities are appearing more and more frequently (e.g., Miller 1986). Further, it is not difficult to see how the affirmation of the collective unconscious opens up possibilities for reinterpretation of such currently embattled questions as "how God acts" among and upon us, how "revelation" may be understood to take place, and how the power of the Scriptural witness may be better understood and interpreted.

If any depth-psychological view is taken seriously, then, the whole theological enterprise has to be rethought in terms of its nature, its sources, its methods, its meanings, and its affirmations. As noted above, this is inevitable, for depth psychology constitutes a revolution in the understanding of human being and thereby affects every distinctively human enterprise. Some theologians may conclude that the judgment that there are powerful unconscious psychic factors at work in human beings is unsound. If they do so prior to careful study of the depth-psychological claims, however, they will be doing so prejudicially and irresponsibly, in a manner reminiscent of the repudiations of Galileo's observations by persons unaware of the telescope! Unconscious factors are, obviously, more difficult to demonstrate, so one may safely anticipate that there will continue to be major disagreements among modern theologians regarding this subject. The influence of depth psychology upon theology is growing, however, and awareness of the issues involved will be increasingly important for understanding theological proposals and debates.

WORKS CITED

Freud, S.
   1938   *The Basic Writings of Sigmund Freud*. Translated and edited by A. A. Brill. New York: Modern Library.

   1949   *A General Introduction to Psychoanalysis*. Translated by Joan Riviere. New York: Perma Giants.

   1960   *The Ego and the Id*. Translated and edited by James Strachey. New York: W. W. Norton.

   1965   *New Introductory Lectures on Psychoanalysis*. Translated and edited by James Strachey. New York: W. W. Norton.

Jones, E.
   1963   *The Life and Work of Sigmund Freud*. 1-vol. ed., edited and abridged by Lionel Trilling and Steven Marcus. Garden City, N.Y.: Doubleday Anchor Books.

Jung, C. G.
    1955   *The Symbolic Life: Miscellaneous Writings*. The Collected Works
                    of C. G. Jung, vol. 18. Bollingen Series XX, 2d ed. Princeton:
                    Princeton University Press.

    1961   *Memories, Dreams, Reflections*. Recorded and edited by Aniela
                    Jaffe. Translated by Richard Winston and Clara Winston. Vin-
                    tage Books. New York: Random House.

    1964   "Approaching the Unconscious." In *Man and His Symbols*,
                    C. G. Jung, M.-L. von Franz, J. L. Henderson, J. Jacobi,
                    Aniela Jaffe, 1–94. A Laurel Edition. Garden City, N.Y.:
                    Doubleday & Co.

    1966   *The Practice of Psychotherapy*. The Collected Works of C. G.
                    Jung, vol. 16. 2d ed.

    1968a   *The Archetypes of the Collective Unconscious*. The Collected
                    Works of C. G. Jung, vol. 9, part 1. 2d ed.

    1968b   *Aion: Researches into the Phenomenology of the Self*. The Col-
                    lected Works of C. G. Jung, vol. 9, part 2. 2d ed.

    1969   *The Structure and Dynamics of the Psyche*. The Collected Works
                    of C. G. Jung, vol. 8, 2d ed.

Miller, D. L.
    1986   *Three Faces of God: Traces of the Trinity in Literature and Life*.
                    Philadelphia: Fortress Press.

Progoff, I.
    1956   *The Death and Rebirth of Psychology*. New York: Julian Press.

Rizzuto, A.
    1979   *The Birth of the Living God*. Chicago: University of Chicago
                    Press.

Watson, R. I.
    1968   *The Great Psychologists: From Aristotle to Freud*. 2d ed. Philadel-
                    phia and New York: J. B. Lippincott.

5

REDISCOVERING THE BIBLICAL WORLDS

The Development of Modern Biblical Criticism

AMONG THE SEVERAL revolutions that have contributed to the character of the world in which theologians seek to interpret the Christian faith, that which has had the greatest and most direct impact upon theology has been the development of biblical criticism. Its rise was made both possible and inevitable by the other aspects of the growth of the modern world that I have sought to suggest in the foregoing sketches of modern science, philosophy, and depth psychology. As already noted, the scientific developments challenged the authority of both church and Scripture, for they provided a new and persuasive basis for obtaining knowledge, including conclusions contrary to some that had been understood to be the teachings of Scripture. Gradually, but with an ever-increasing frequency, questions were raised concerning the traditional beliefs regarding the nature of the books of the Bible. At the root of those questions was the suggestion—which was to become a conviction—that those books are historical documents showing the characteristics of human authorship. As long as it was assumed that the Bible was essentially the product of divine authorship inerrantly setting forth the Word of God for every generation, such questions as how, when, and where the particular books came to be were not very important. In a sense these questions had been raised during the second, third, and fourth centuries when the Christian church found it necessary to determine which documents would be regarded as authoritative, in part by judging which were "apostolic." These questions were not raised in the way they are in modern biblical criticism, however, and once the canon had been determined, it was believed that the Holy Spirit had guided the church in its determination. Consequently those questions lost their importance.

That for many centuries the divine authority of the Bible was so firmly believed as to eliminate any concern with historical settings and human perspectives in its books did not mean, however, that there was any such thorough agreement on how the Bible should be interpreted. It is probably safe to say that there never has been a period in the history of Christianity during which there was not significant disagreement within the church concerning the proper interpretation of the Scriptures, though particular views have attained dominance from time to time. Familiar examples would include: (1) the conflict between the followers of the school of Alexandria who insisted upon an allegorical or symbolic interpretation of most texts and the followers of the school of Antioch which demanded a literal or historical interpretation of most texts; (2) the medieval disagreements over how many different meanings each text has (some argued for three, some for four, some for seven, etc.); and (3) the contrast between Luther's sense of freedom to evaluate and even criticize books of the Bible and to interpret its texts nonliterally and Calvin's insistence upon the equal and divine authority of every text.

Nevertheless, even though it is not true that before the modern era there was always—within Christendom—a common understanding of how the Scriptures should be interpreted, it is possible to specify broad general contrasts between the judgments of the modern biblical scholars and those of the interpreters throughout the earlier centuries of the church's history. During that long history a theological belief governed the approach to scriptural interpretation, the belief that the real author of all canonical books was God and that since Jesus Christ was and is God's final self-revelation, all of Scripture speaks primarily of him. On this theological basis little need was seen for study of the historical and cultural settings or origins of the texts.

By contrast, modern biblical criticism is rooted in the judgment that the biblical writings can be approached "historically."

> In place of the unhistorical attitude which saw the Bible as a vast harmonious complex of prophecy and fulfillment, type and anti-type, allegorical picture and spiritual reality, fused together by the uniform inspiration of the Holy Spirit, Biblical criticism sought to recover the true and original meaning of the literal sense, and to set the various documents comprising the Bible in their proper context in history instead of seeing them as pieces fixed unalterably in a divinely planned mosaic pattern of Holy Scripture. (Lampe and Woolcombe 1957, 15)

Thus to approach the books of the Bible "historically" meant, among other things, to take seriously the historical and cultural settings in which they were produced. This does not seem at all revolutionary until it is recognized that it was an expression of the judgment that the biblical literature could and should be studied in the same way that any other literature is studied without either the methods or the results being controlled by either theological doctrines or ecclesiastical authorities. This, in turn, entailed another judgment that has not always been explicit, namely that one must take seriously the humanness of the biblical authors.

To state these judgments in this general form is oversimplifying and potentially misleading. They did not appear suddenly in any fully articulated manner, but were the result of a very slow process whose every step was challenged by the traditional views.

THE BEGINNING OF HISTORICAL-CRITICAL
APPROACHES TO THE OLD TESTAMENT

The gradual development of historical-critical approaches to the Bible can be seen in the history of studies of the Pentateuch (the first five books of the Old Testament). The firmly held traditional view was that these books had all been written by Moses. Texts in Deuteronomy (such as 1:1 and 4:44–45) gave support to this belief, and it is the evident assumption of New Testament authors. Doubts about this tradition were raised from time to time on various grounds, such as that Moses could not have attributed to God such things as swearing. Some noted that the style does not change with the end of the Pentateuch as one would expect with the end of Moses' authorship, and others pointed to repetitions and contradictions that would indicate more than a single author.

> Thus Ibn Ezra (d. 1167) hints with regard to Gen. xii, 6, that the addition *The Canaanites were then in the land* to the sentence *And Abram journeyed through the land as far as the place Shechem, as far as the terebinth of the soothsayer* must come from a period when the Canaanites were no longer in the land, in other words a period which lay a considerable time after Moses. Carlstadt . . . notes . . . in 1520, that Moses could not have compiled the five books named after him, since it is nonsensical to ascribe to him the account of his own death which appears in Deut. xxxiv, 5–12, and that this account in fact reveals the same style as the preceding narrative. Attention was drawn to the various repetitions and contradictions and other literary defects of all kinds, particularly by Andreas Masius (1574), Isaac de la Peyrere (1655), and Richard Simon, and they drew from this the conclusion that the Pentateuch as we now have it could not have come from Moses, but was the work of a later author, who certainly made use of notes by Moses, but added to them a great deal from other sources as well as material of his own. (Eissfeldt 1965, 159–60)

The philosophers Thomas Hobbes (1588–1679) and Baruch Spinoza (1632–77) both argued on the basis of the internal evidence of the books that the Pentateuch could not have been written in its present form until long after the time of Moses. Since the methods of these men were in conflict with the general spirit of their times, both they and their writings were widely condemned. The first theologian to take up the arguments that had been developed and assert that Moses could not have been the author of all of the books traditionally attributed to him was the Roman Catholic biblical scholar Richard Simon (1638–1712). In his *Histoire Critique du Vieux Testament*, forerunner of modern biblical introductions, he sought to show that various Old Testament books could not have been written in the periods that they describe, but were the result of gradual compilation. Although Simon had obtained several appropriate official approvals for the publication of this book, the popular preacher, author, and controversialist Jacques Benigne Bossuet (1627–1704), who was influential at the royal court, condemned it—without having read the actual text—and succeeded in having it suppressed. Simon was expelled from his priestly order (Steinmann 1960, 124–30).

The shift from the question of whether or not Moses could have written the Pentateuch to an attempt to distinguish different component parts underlying those books first appeared in 1711 in a book by a German pastor, H. B. Witter. This book was a commentary on the first twenty-seven chapters of Genesis which pointed out that Gen. 1:1—2:4 used a different name for God than that employed in Gen. 2:5—3:24, and that the contents of these two portions of the book were parallel. This work was scarcely noticed, soon forgotten, and not rediscovered until the twentieth century (Eissfeldt 1965, 160).

Modern source criticism of the Pentateuch was begun by a book published anonymously in 1753 entitled *Conjectures on the Reminiscences Which Moses Appears to Have Used in Composing the Book of Genesis*. Its author was later revealed to be Jean Astruc (1684–1766), a highly respected physician. Astruc began with the question of how Moses could have known so much about events, some of which took place more than twenty-four hundred years before his birth. He noted that Moses could have obtained this information only from revelation or from the reports of those who had been witnesses to the events. As to the possibility of revelation being his source, Astruc argued that although elsewhere in the Pentateuch Moses has indicated when his source was divine inspiration, and the prophets have done the same, nowhere in Genesis is any such claim made, so it should be judged that his sources were human traditions. This judgment he saw to be supported by such things as repetitions and chronological displacements in the texts and by the pattern in which two different names for God are used. He drew attention to the fact that these names, *Jahweh (Jehovah)* and *Elohim*, are not simply alternatives used indiscriminately for each other—each is employed in separate and distinctive passages.

On the basis of such observations, Astruc concluded that the Book of Genesis involves the mingling of different records, and he sought to distinguish those sources. He first separated those sections that used *Elohim* as the divine name and those that used *Jahweh (Jehovah)*, believing that he thus obtained a clear indication of the fragments that belonged to the two main sources used by Moses. He also found that there were fragments that belonged to neither of these, possibly as many as ten additional sources being involved.

Astruc's contention that the evidence found within the Book of Genesis shows that book to be dependent upon earlier documents might well have been ignored and forgotten had it not been for the work of J. G. Eichhorn (1752–1827). In his *Introduction to the Old Testament* (1st ed., 1780–83) he took up Astruc's description of the *Elohim* and *Jahweh (Jehovah)* documents and further distinguished the two in terms of their characteristic content and style. It was this work that made the demonstration of the existence of the two written sources of Genesis persuasive in the eyes of the scholars. Although at first accepting the assumption of Moses' authorship, Eichhorn later concluded that the two main sources and several additional fragments were edited into the Book of Genesis by a later redactor (Eissfeldt 1965, 162).

Thus began a long and continuing history of scholarly attempts to discern and distinguish the various sources that lie behind the books of the Pentateuch (and also other books of the Old Testament). Many different proposals have been made of the number of documents and/or fragments, what belongs to each one, and when each should be dated. The best-known and long the most influential of these theories is often called the Graf-Wellhausen hypothesis, so-named for the two scholars whose work brought this proposal into its "final" form. This interpretation distinguished four principal documents underlying the composition of the Pentateuch. These were designated "J" (for the use of the divine name "Jehovah" or "Jahweh"), believed to have originated in southern Judea in the tenth century B.C.E.; "E" (for the use of the divine name "Elohim"), a document formulated about the eighth century B.C.E. from a northern tradition; "D," which constituted the source of chapters 12—26 of Deuteronomy and the basis of Josiah's reform in 621 B.C.E.; and "P," a "Priestly" document formulated after the Babylonian Exile (commonly dated 586–538 B.C.E.).

Although scholars today place much less confidence in the reliability of the details of any particular theory regarding the number of documents and fragments and the dating of these, they remain convinced that the internal evidence of these biblical books shows them to have resulted from a long historical process involving several stages of compiling and editing. The kinds of data upon which they base this conclusion are basically the same as those pointed to in the work of Astruc and Eichhorn.

The form of historical research that we have been discussing here is com-

monly called *source criticism* or *literary criticism*. Its searches for a fuller understanding of the nature, sources, and development of the books of the Bible
have been supplemented by several other kinds of historical-critical research.
Prominent among these are *form criticism*, a method for discerning oral units
of tradition that preceded the written sources; *tradition criticism*, the study of
the ways in which the traditions adapted to new situations as they were reaf-
firmed during the continuing history of the Hebrew peoples; *redaction criticism*, studies focusing upon the distinctive contributions made to the developments of the traditions by the "editors" who brought those traditions into
the forms in which they come to us (or into any of the earlier formulations
that can be reconstructed); *textual criticism*, studies of the varieties of texts for
a book or passage of Scripture upon which today's translations and versions
are based in an effort to establish the most probable original text; *canon criticism*, studies of the historical processes by which the Hebrew and Christian
canons (lists of the writings that are to be judged to constitute the official
Scriptures) were determined; and several others. The following sections seek
to explain and illustrate the uses of several methods of historical-critical
biblical scholarship in connection with portions of the New Testament.

HISTORICAL-CRITICAL APPROACHES
TO THE NEW TESTAMENT

One might expect that because of the more recent date of the books of the
New Testament, and because of the far-shorter period during which its several writings were produced, there would be fewer and simpler problems
than in the case of Old Testament study. Although there are differences for
these reasons, the problems remain very complex. The application of the
methods of historical-critical research to the New Testament will be illustrated here in relation to the Gospels and the letters of Saint Paul.

Problems with the Traditional
View of the Gospels

As one might expect, a major focus of these studies has been upon the Gospels and the question of our knowledge of Jesus. As long as it was assumed
that the biblical books were divinely guaranteed to be inerrant, it was also assumed that the four accounts of the ministry and teaching of Jesus in the Gospels could be readily harmonized. The supposition that these books were
simple, objective accounts based upon eyewitness reports was supported
by the belief that Matthew and John were written by the disciples of those
names, and that Mark's information came directly from Peter and Luke's

from Paul. That these names were added later to anonymous writings was only learned relatively recently.

It was recognized early in the history of the church that there are literary relationships among the Gospels. The "orthodox" theory concerning those relationships can be traced back at least as far as Augustine (354–430). He taught that the four Gospels were written in the sequence, Matthew, Mark, Luke, and John, and that each successive writer had knowledge of the earlier writings. He judged Mark to be an abridgment of Matthew, Luke to have used both, and John all three.

Putting together a single self-consistent account of the course of Jesus' ministry is not as easy, however, as the traditional assumptions imply. Difficulties are apparent as soon as one compares the accounts in John with those in the other three. For example, Matthew, Mark, and Luke indicate that Jesus' public ministry began after the arrest of John the Baptist (Matt. 4:12–17; Mark 1:14; Luke 3:19ff.), while John reports a period of simultaneous ministry by Jesus and John the Baptist (John 3:22–24). The first three Gospels report only one trip by Jesus to Jerusalem (apart from Luke's account of the childhood trip), whereas John records several (John 2:13; 5:1; 7:10; 12:12). The former books tell of Jesus' final visit to Jerusalem lasting about a week, whereas in John Jesus is described as being in and about Jerusalem from the Feast of Tabernacles until his death at the time of the Passover— about six months. The indication of Matthew, Mark, and Luke is that the duration of Jesus' public ministry was about one year, but John's account requires more than two years. There is also disagreement as to the date of Jesus' crucifixion, for the information given in Matt. 26:17, Mark 14:12, and Luke 22:7 places Jesus' death on the fifteenth of Nisan, whereas John 18:28 and 19:14, 31 place the crucifixion on the day of preparation, the fourteenth of Nisan. To these and many other differences in detail, one may add the marked contrast in the style of Jesus' teaching between the accounts in John and those in the first three Gospels.

That there are such differences in the accounts given in the four Gospels did not go unnoticed until the modern era. Luther, for example, made the following comment upon the observation that the cleansing of the temple is reported as coming at the beginning of Jesus' ministry in John's Gospel, but at the end in the others: "The Gospels follow no order in recording the acts and miracles of Jesus, and the matter is not, after all, of much importance. If a difficulty arises in regard to the Holy Scripture and we cannot solve it, we must just let it alone" (Schweitzer 1945, 13). By contrast, Andreas Osiander (1498–1552) "maintained the principle that if an event is recorded more than once in the Gospels, in different connections, it happened more than once and in different connections." Albert Schweitzer noted that this would mean that the daughter of Jairus was raised from the dead several times (ibid., 13).

Attempts to harmonize the teachings of the four Gospels concerning the life of Jesus ordinarily tried to fit the material from the first three into the chronological framework found in John, since it contained the longer time span. However, the primacy of John for gaining historical understanding of Jesus was effectively attacked by David Friedrich Strauss (1808–74). In his *Life of Jesus* (1st ed., 1835, 1836) Strauss took great pains to show that the Fourth Gospel is dominated by a theological perspective and by the aim to address particular misunderstandings of the Gospel, and that processes that had just begun in the other three Gospels were here at a more advanced stage (Schweitzer 1945, 85ff.). This work was met with a storm of protest that ended Strauss's chances for a promising academic career. It was attacked by most theologians, and it evoked several more conservative "Lives of Jesus." With support at important points from subsequent works by F. C. Baur (1792–1860), however, the judgment that the Gospel of John is further removed from the events of the historical Jesus than the accounts in the first three Gospels was to become the dominant view. This in turn produced a greatly increased amount of critical attention to the relationships among Matthew, Mark, and Luke.

The Synoptic Problem

The first three Gospels had been called "the Synoptic Gospels" since late in the eighteenth century because of the recognition that there is so much common material in them. It is not simply that the same narratives appear many times in all three, but that the identity of these narratives often includes the very language employed. On the other hand, there are also decided differences among the three. Matthew and Luke include more detail at the beginning and end than does Mark, but do not agree with each other in this material. For example, their genealogies of Jesus differ, and while Matthew reports resurrection appearances in both Jerusalem and Galilee, Luke reports them only in and around Jerusalem. Yet there is also material in Matthew and Luke that is virtually identical, and which is not in Mark. There is other material in each of the three that is not found in any of the others. The "Synoptic Problem" has been *how to account for the extensive similarities among the three while also accounting for the differences*. The evidence seems clear enough that there are literary dependencies among them, but just what is the nature of these dependencies?

When this problem was clearly recognized in the latter half of the eighteenth century, several theories developed as possible solutions. The one that was to become generally accepted is that Mark is a primary source for both Matthew and Luke. This conclusion is supported by several observations derived from an analysis of the three Gospels. First, about 95 percent of the material in Mark is paralleled in Matthew or Luke or in both. More specifically, only three of the eighty-eight paragraphs in Mark are absent from both Matthew and Luke. About 65 percent of Matthew is paralleled in one or both of the others, and 53 percent of Luke is so paralleled. In effect, as Floyd V. Filson pointed out, of all the things that Jesus must have said and done during a ministry lasting probably more than two years, these three Gospels report only a few hours worth of teaching and enough deeds to fill but a few weeks, and they chose the same few sayings and actions (Filson 1971, 1130).

In addition, this common material is largely ordered in the same sequences. There is one event that is placed differently in each of the three Gospels. Otherwise the order found in Mark is usually followed when the same event is reported in one or both of the others, and Matthew and Luke never agree against Mark (ibid.). In fact, "the agreement between Matthew and Luke begins where Mark begins, and ends where Mark ends" (Perry 1951, 62).

There is also extensive agreement in wording in spite of the fact that the distinctive style of each author is discernible. In parallel passages Matthew and Luke employ the exact words used in Mark more than half the time. Filson points out that this is not accounted for by the theory that all three reported the exact words of Jesus, first because it is also true of the descriptions of events, and second because Jesus taught in Aramaic, and these agreements are in Greek. No two translators will independently choose exactly the same words and word orders that often (Filson 1971, 1130). Yet the common word choice and word order include both unusual words and awkward Greek constructions (Perry 1951, 63). Here again there is more agreement between Mark and each of the others than there is between Matthew and Luke and a very small amount of agreement of these two against Mark.

The great amount of data represented in these summary statements has led most New Testament scholars to the conclusion that there is a close literary relationship among these three Gospels, and that Mark was a primary source for both Matthew and Luke.

This leaves a further important literary relationship to be explained—there are some two hundred verses that are present in Matthew and Luke in very similar form that are not present in Mark. The same kinds of observations about these verses have led many scholars to the conclusion that Matthew and Luke had another common source that has been designated "Q." The alternative hypothesis would be that either Matthew or Luke used the other Gospel as a source, and few scholars have found this proposal persuasive (ibid., 64).

Thus a two-source theory became the generally accepted solution to the problem of the similarities and differences of the first three Gospels. That is, the nature of these similarities has been explained on the theory that both Matthew and Luke employed Mark as a primary source, and that both Matthew and Luke employed another source (Q) that is now lost. In addition Matthew and Luke each had other material on which to draw, thus accounting for materials found in only one of them. Although various attacks have been mounted against this theory, and there are increasing warnings that it oversimplifies our understandings of the relationships among the Synoptic Gospels, the majority of historical-critical biblical scholars continue to regard this theory as the basic answer to the Synoptic problem.

The Origin and Nature of Mark

The two-source theory does not, however, constitute a full explanation of the origin of the Gospels, most obviously because it does not deal at all with the origin of Mark. The initial and general assumption when the priority of Mark was established was that Mark was a basically simple historical account putting us in almost direct touch with the life and teachings of Jesus. This understanding of Mark was strongly attacked as early as 1841 in the work of Bruno Bauer, but his conclusions were largely ignored, and the comforting assumption of Mark's historicity persisted until the early twentieth century when a series of studies showed its untenability.

Something of a sensation was created in German-speaking theological circles when Wilhelm Wrede's *Das Messiasgeheimnis in den Evangelien* (The messianic secret in the gospels) was published in 1901. Wrede attacked the way in which both conservative and liberal scholars were treating Mark as a biography of Jesus. He sought to show that both were reading into Mark connections and developments that are not in the text. The liberals, for example, were claiming to trace a development of Jesus' "messianic consciousness" through the course of the Markan accounts.

Wrede pointed out that throughout Mark there is a tension between the continuing theme that Jesus' messiahship was a secret until his resurrection and the further teaching that his messiahship was revealed to the disciples (and to others) who, nevertheless, did not understand. Both sides of this tension are, in Wrede's judgment, rooted in the conviction that real understanding of who Jesus was could only begin with the resurrection. He further argued that the very earliest understanding of Jesus' messiahship was that it in fact began with the resurrection, contending that if the church had had an earlier belief that Jesus was Messiah during his earthly life, it would never have occurred to anyone to suppose that its beginning came only with the resurrection. Yet, there is clear evidence for the very early belief that he became Messiah after his death.

In Wrede's view it was only natural that the church, once it had come into being on the basis of its acknowledgment of the risen Lord as Messiah, would begin to interpret its recollections of the earthly Jesus in terms of its faith in the resurrected Jesus as Messiah. The concept of the messianic secret arose during the transition period when there was no known claim of being the Messiah on the part of the earthly Jesus, but when the church was increasingly recalling that earthly life in terms of its postresurrection faith.

Wrede thus contended that the messianic secret was a concept employed by the evangelist (Markan redactor) to deal with the problem of traditions, on the one hand, that did not include an affirmation or recognition of Jesus as Messiah before his resurrection, and, on the other hand, the perception of Jesus as Messiah by the church and the concern to proclaim Jesus as Messiah in this Gospel.

Two very important interrelated points are being made here by Wrede. One is that the Gospel of Mark is not a biographical account of Jesus' life—it shows itself to be a purposeful arranging of traditions that do not in fact include the kind of detailed knowledge of sequences and motivations required for a biography. The other is that the purpose and arranging are very theological. That is, the evangelist has presented the material in terms of his theological perspective and with a theological aim. Both of these contentions deny the possibility of treating Mark as a simple and direct reporting of the life and teaching of Jesus.

Wrede was not denying the possibility of gaining valid knowledge of Jesus from the Gospel of Mark; he saw a variety of genuinely historical points in Mark that are not distorted by Mark's theologizing. But, argued Wrede, it is the theological interpretation that provides the basic motivation, color, and pattern of the portrayal, so that the Gospel is not a biography so much as part of the history of doctrine (Wrede 1971, 131). Wrede's book produced a great deal of reaction, most of which was negative. Today many scholars disagree with his explanation of the messianic secret, but further studies have increasingly corroborated his two general conclusions that the Gospel of Mark is dependent upon prior traditions and deeply influenced by the evangelist's theological convictions and purposes. J. Wellhausen showed that there were stages in the traditions and sequences of traditions that were brought together by an editorial process to produce the Gospel of Mark, so that Mark and the other Gospels are primarily sources for understanding the history of the early church, and only indirectly sources for knowledge of the life of Jesus (Robinson 1959, 35).

K. L. Schmidt provided for many an adequate justification for this approach to the Gospels in a book published in 1919. He showed that if Mark is treated as history, various passages are inconsistent with the structure or framework in which the story is presented. The inconsistencies include both the geographical and the chronological references. He concluded that the overall structure of the Gospel is not itself historical. It is rather a contribution of the evangelist that organizes the various traditions into a unified proclamation (Schmidt 1919). The general effect of this study was to make it clear that although it might be possible to have knowledge of particular events in the life of Jesus, an understanding of their historical sequence is ruled out by the nature of the sources (ibid., 317).

Form Criticism of the Synoptic Gospels

This limitation has been further emphasized by the application of form criticism to the Gospels. In the study of the Gospels, as in the study of the Pentateuch, the work of source criticism in searching for evidence of the documents that preceded our present books led beyond such documents to oral traditions. This was much less surprising in the case of the Pentateuch where such an enormous time span is involved between some of the events reported there and the time when its books might be supposed first to have been written. Indeed, one must ask when writing first began among the people with whom those accounts are concerned. The latter question is not present in New Testament times, and the time between the events and the writing of the Gospels is very brief by comparison. That there was a gap is, however, clear and hardly surprising. As far as anyone knows, Jesus wrote nothing. The earliest Christian community had no need for written records both because there were among them those who had witnessed and participated in the events, and because they expected God to end this world with the final judgment and the establishment of the kingdom very soon.

The problems posed by the failure of this expectation can be seen reflected in the earliest of the New Testament documents, 1 Thessalonians (probably written about 50 C.E.). Grief had arisen in that congregation because some of the faithful had died while Christ had not yet returned. Paul wrote to instruct and reassure them:

> For this we declare to you by the word of the Lord, that we who are alive, who are left until the coming of the Lord, shall not precede those who have fallen asleep. For the Lord himself will descend from heaven with a cry of command, with the archangel's call, and with the sound of the trumpet of God. And the

dead in Christ will rise first; then we who are alive, who are left, shall be caught up together with them in the clouds to meet the Lord in the air; and so we shall always be with the Lord. Therefore comfort one another with these words. (1 Thess. 4:15–18, RSV)

It was one to two decades after this letter before the earliest of our Gospels was composed, and the gap between the earthly life of Jesus and that writing involved much more than time. Alfred M. Perry has described it as follows:

It is a far cry from Galilee to Ephesus or Rome. A generation or more has passed. In the interval the simple village and country life of Palestine has given way to the heat of the crowded industrialized cities. The Aramaic tongue of the Galilean peasant has been replaced by the Greek dialect common to most of the Mediterranean world. The tales and reminiscences passed from mouth to mouth by intimate friends have at last become written records, and finally books to be published to the world at large. The Christian message has passed from the hands of Jews to Gentiles whose past religious experience had been rooted in the innumerable faiths of the Hellenistic age. The informal group of intimate followers of Jesus has grown into a great family of churches in all the larger cities, strong enough to begin to attract the suspicious attention of the mighty empire. And the Jesus, who had once in Galilee seemed but a teacher and leader, is now proclaimed as Messiah and Lord and Son of God.

In short the tradition of Jesus has leaped every cultural barrier—of language, nationality, religion, theology, and way of life. The query is inevitable: By what channels was it transplanted? And a second question follows: How much was it transformed in the process? (Perry 1951, 60–61)

Form criticism is directly concerned with these questions. It judges that in large measure the materials that we now have in the Gospels crossed these several barriers in small units which were first handed on orally and which were commonly in rather stereotyped forms.

In order to illustrate the meaning and importance of such an observation for the biblical interpreter, Gene M. Tucker suggested that we try to imagine a prominent pastor of an earlier generation who has left behind him a large unorganized collection of papers including prayers, sermons, addresses, lectures, class lessons, letters of various kinds, and so forth. Later, if someone decides to write about the life and work of this pastor, it will be necessary to determine, insofar as possible, the kind of material represented by each document, for much misunderstanding will result if one supposes that a statement addressed to a Sunday school class was addressed to God or that a joke told in an after-dinner speech was intended as a factual report to the bishop. Therefore attention will be paid to such things as stereotyped formulas—"Dear Sir," "Ladies and Gentlemen," "Sincerely yours," "Almighty God," or "Once upon a time . . ." (Tucker 1971, 10).

Such a technique of identifying the individual units of oral or written tradition, classifying them according to form, and inferring the "life situations" in the early church in and for which these forms and traditions functioned was first applied to the Synoptic Gospels by Martin Dibelius in 1919 in *Die Form-geschichte des Evangeliums* (the title of the 1935 translation of the revised 2d ed. is *From Tradition to Gospel*) and then by Rudolph Bultmann in 1921 in *Geschichte der synoptischen Tradition* (the title of the 1963 English translation of the 3d German ed. of 1957 is *History of the Synoptic Tradition*). Their work evoked much protest, was long controversial, and even today gives rise to some strong reactions. One reason for these negative responses is that the results of their studies indicated that objective information about Jesus is even more difficult to obtain than had until then been supposed.

This relative skepticism concerning knowledge of Jesus results in part from the form-critical finding that the particular units of the tradition manifest far more of the interests and the problems of the early Christian community in which the forms developed than concern with giving objective reporting of the life and teaching of Jesus. It is sometimes said that the form critics *assume* this to be true, but it is not a simple assumption. It is a judgment based upon a study of the texts that has led to the effort to show this influence of the settings in the life of the early church to be important. The early church was not involved in historical science but in preaching, teaching, worship, controversy, and apologetics. The recollections and reports concerning Jesus' words and deeds were quite naturally repeated in terms of these activities and needs. It is judged that in this process certain standard forms developed that were adapted to the typical situations in the life of the church.

This process may be illustrated by reference to Bultmann's treatment of Mark 2:23–28 and 3:1–6, the stories of the disciples plucking grain on the Sabbath and of the Sabbath healing of the man with the withered hand. These passages were classified by Bultmann as instances of "Conflict and Didactic Sayings," a subdivision of "Apophthegms" (short, terse sayings or maxims, in a brief narrative setting) (Bultmann 1963, 11–27, 39–54). After examining several such accounts of controversies, Bultmann sought to show the common features of the typical form and further to show their similarity to stories of rabbinic disputes. That there are many such "controversy dialogues" in the Gospels structured according to a common stylized form, a form already familiar in the Palestinian setting, was interpreted by Bultmann as clear evidence that these were not simple unadorned and undeveloped reports of objective events in the life of Jesus. Rather are they to be seen as manifesting a development of the tradition significantly influenced by the settings and concerns of the early church. Further, Bultmann saw the strong similarity to the stories of rabbinic disputes as indicating that these conflict dialogues developed in this form in the Palestinian setting of the early church rather than in the more Hellenized settings. The setting is to be seen as more specific than that, however, for these dialogues and disputes relate consistently to questions concerning the Law. Bultmann's study concluded that their formation in the early church developed in a context of discussions about the Law both within the church and between the church and its critics. That is to say, the *form* in which these accounts came to be more or less fixed in the developing tradition was a result of the need of the early church to answer questions about the relations of Christians to the Judaic Law. The recollections and reports of Jesus' teachings and deeds and of the general impact of his life and ministry were being employed by the church in relation to its present struggles.

Careful study of the many conflict dialogues in the Gospels revealed further common characteristics that supported the view that the tradition was being formed under the impact of the early church settings. For example, as in the story of the disciples plucking grain on the Sabbath, several conflict dialogues deal with attacks on the disciples rather than on Jesus. Bultmann pointed out that there are several features of these accounts that do not fit well with the supposition that they are simple reports of events in the lives of Jesus and the disciples. In these stories the disciples are defended by Jesus when they are accused of plucking grain on the Sabbath, not fasting as John's disciples did, and eating with unwashed hands. Are we to suppose, then, that Jesus was quite "proper" in all these respects, while his disciples were not? Or might it be that his opponents were afraid to make a direct charge against Jesus and therefore only criticized his disciples? How then would that fit with the reports of direct attacks upon him, such as when he healed on the Sabbath? Bultmann's conclusion was that in these reports of attacks upon the disciples who were then defended by Jesus the *form* of these accounts as they come to us is indicative of the fact that the immediate purpose of these accounts in the life of the early church (when the form was determined) was to defend the conduct of early Christian communities against attacks on their conduct by appealing to the authority of Jesus Christ (ibid., 48).

This conclusion that the traditions were modified in terms of the situation of the early church during the course of their transmission was not intended to suggest that these accounts have no relationship to Jesus' own life and teaching. It does suggest, however, that one must be much more cautious in making assertions about the historical Jesus because of such factors in the development of the tradition. Bultmann's own conclusion about the relation of these controversy dialogues to Jesus was that the decisive saying attributed to

Jesus is the portion most likely to have originated in Jesus' own life and teaching (ibid., 49).

This is the reason Bultmann classified the controversy dialogues under the broader category or form of "apophthegms." It is the brief pointed saying that is the heart of the story—"The sabbath was made for man, not man for the sabbath" (Mark 2:27) and "Is it lawful on the sabbath to do good or to do harm, to save life or to kill?" (Mark 3:4)—in the passages we are noting as examples.

Another characteristic Bultmann saw emerging from the study of the controversy dialogues was that there was a growing tendency in the development of the tradition during the life of the early church to identify Jesus' opponents as the scribes and the Pharisees. This identification of the Pharisees is present in the two examples from Mark 2 and 3, they being those who ask Jesus about the disciples' unlawful plucking of grain on the Sabbath (Mark 2:24), and those identified at the end of the story of the healing of the man with the withered hand: "The Pharisees went out, and immediately held counsel with the Herodians against him, how to destroy him" (Mark 3:6). It is Bultmann's judgment that this last verse is "secondary," that is, that it was added to the tradition in the process of development. He notes that in Q (the source of the common material in Matthew and Luke that is not found in Mark) the source of the opposition is unnamed, as for example in Luke 11:16, whereas in the parallel in Matt. 12:38 the unnamed challengers of Luke (from Q) are named as the scribes and Pharisees, and in Mark 8:11f. the secondary character of this identification is even more evident. Bultmann supported this contention by considering a large number of other texts, noting that this tendency was present not only in the Palestinian settings, but also in the Hellenistic world where the historical relationships of scribes, Pharisees, Sadducees, and high priests were no longer known (Bultmann 1963, 52–53). What was at work was a tendency of the tradition, not a matter of simple historical fact, for while scribes and Pharisees were surely among Jesus' opponents,

> it will not do to think of the Scribes and Pharisees as an exclusive opposition to Jesus and the Early Church. They are only seen in this light as a result of the gospel Tradition. The distinction between those who did and those who did not believe on the Messiah in the Palestinian Church must be seen as something quite different from that between Pharisee and non-Pharisee. There were differences amongst the Pharisees themselves, and there were some Pharisees inside the Church. (Ibid., 53)

It should be clear even from such brief illustrative sketches that the form-critical studies of the influences of the early church upon the development of the gospel traditions cast doubt upon the previously supposed authenticity of many New Testament accounts of the life and teachings of Jesus. Bultmann's work in particular has been seen as extremely skeptical in this regard. It is not uncommon to see the statement that Bultmann regarded the effort to obtain knowledge of the historical Jesus as both impossible and illegitimate. This, however, is clearly an overstatement. It is nevertheless true that because of his convictions concerning the role of the early church in the formation of the tradition, Bultmann insisted upon the importance of recognizing how difficult it is to distinguish the "historical Jesus" from the influences of the witnesses in the texts as we now have them. Something of Bultmann's own convictions about Jesus in spite of the historical-critical problems can be seen in the following statement, which appears in his discussion of these controversy dialogues.

> So in the end the question can very well be put, whether the Tradition has not repressed the prophetic-apocalyptic character of the mission of Jesus in favour of his activity as a Rabbi. . . . Yet in face of the entire content of the Tradition it can hardly be doubted that Jesus did teach as a Rabbi, gather disciples and engage in disputations. The individual controversy dialogues may not be historical reports of particular incidents in the life of Jesus, but the general character of his life is rightly portrayed in them, on the basis of historical recollection. (Ibid., 50)

Such a qualified affirmation of the New Testament texts as sources for knowledge of the life and teachings of Jesus is very disturbing to those who have assumed that the Gospel accounts can simply be taken at face value, so it is hardly surprising that form criticism has given rise to much opposition. One must distinguish here between popular opposition and scholarly opposition, however. In theological matters the former is usually a matter of emotion, but anyone who has any notions of functioning as a scholar knows that what one has assumed and what one wants to believe are not relevant against the evidence. More important, one must distinguish here between opposition to form criticism itself and opposition to particular conclusions of particular form critics, such as Bultmann. To use the methods of form criticism in the study of the Gospels does entail the judgment that the texts manifest influences of the early church settings within which the tradition was formed, but it does not predetermine what conclusions one may reach about just what those influences were and how much they may impede the search for historical knowledge of the original events. Even Bultmann and Dibelius differed considerably in their conclusions on these questions, and many New Testament scholars have employed the methods of form criticism in defense of conclusions differing from those of both of these pioneers. Indeed, in the several decades since their first form-critical studies were published those methods have come to be recognized as being among the essential tools of New Testament scholarship. The extent to which they can be used fruitfully continues to be a matter of debate, but as W. D. Davies has said, "it should be recognized that all serious students of the New Testament today are to some extent Form Critics" (McKnight 1969, 3).

Redaction Criticism of the Synoptic Gospels

The success of the form critics in tracing the history of the Christian tradition prepared the way for the more recent development of New Testament redaction criticism. Redaction criticism is concerned with the coming together of the materials that have gone into the development of the books rather than with the tracing back of those materials as in source criticism (also called literary criticism) and form criticism. It focuses upon the role of the redactors. The term "redactor," which is roughly the same as "editor" or "compiler," refers to those persons who have gathered and reshaped the documents, fragments, oral traditions, etc., into a new unified form at any of the stages at which this may have been done in the history of the books as we now have them. It is thus concerned with literary developments, and it seeks to discern just what role has been played by the redactor in organizing and editing the materials. Judging that each time such an act of compiling, editing, and organizing was done it was done with a purpose related to a particular community and its needs, the redaction critics seek to determine these purposes, communities, and needs in order to understand the development of these texts more fully.

Although this critical focus has only emerged as a major emphasis in New Testament scholarship since the Second World War, its practice can be seen at least as early as Wrede's book on the messianic secret (1901), for that study revealed the theological work of the evangelist "Mark." The development of such an approach was delayed, however, during the period in which more conservative scholars sought to defend the assumption that Mark, as the major source for both Matthew and Luke, is a document giving direct and accurate access to the life and teachings of Jesus, and the form critics carried out the studies that showed that assumption to be untenable. The position of the former did not include any place for creative theological work on the part of "Mark," and the focus of the latter was not upon unifying the tradition's materials by the redactor but upon tracing back the elements in the tradition. In addition there was some tendency among form critics to regard the redactors as mere compilers. The subsequent work of redaction critics has shown, however, that the redactors of the Gospels were genuinely authors who did significant creative theological work in maintaining and developing the

Christian traditions. Indeed, without that creative work done by the evangelist whom we call "Mark," one must wonder what might have prevented an ever-increasing fragmentation of the many distinct units of those traditions.

This focus upon the creative work of the individual evangelists who composed the Gospels means that a third life situation is under examination (Marxsen 1969, 23). The first is the situation of Jesus' own activity, the second the circumstances in the life of the primitive Christian community whose influence form criticism seeks to ascertain, and the third, studied in redaction criticism, the situation in which the evangelists unified these traditions in the form of the Gospels.

Determining the distinctive contributions of the evangelists who composed Matthew and Luke is somewhat easier than in the case of Mark since one can see what they have done with Mark and to a lesser extent the differences in their use of the materials from Q, their other common source. In the case of Mark the possibility of successful redaction-critical work is dependent upon the findings of the form critics concerning the development and the settings of the units of the tradition.

In *What Is Redaction Criticism?* Norman Perrin has given an illustration of this form of New Testament research in a study of the three Synoptic Gospel treatments of the incident at Caesarea Philippi (Perrin 1969, 40–63). On this occasion Jesus is reported to have asked the disciples who people said he was, and, following Mark's version, Peter answered, "You are the Christ." Jesus instructed them to tell no one and then began to teach them concerning the coming sufferings, death, and resurrection of the Son of man. When Peter protested, Jesus rebuked him with the words, "Get behind me, Satan! For you are not on the side of God, but of men." This is followed by Jesus' telling the disciples and the multitude that anyone who would follow him must deny himself and take up his cross, that the Son of man when he comes will be ashamed of anyone who is ashamed of Jesus, and that some who are present will not taste death before they see the kingdom of God come with power (Mark 8:27—9:1, RSV).

By way of preliminary observations, Perrin notes that Mark uses here what is in appearance a story about Jesus and his disciples for the purpose of setting forth what he (Mark) believes the risen Lord has to say to the church in Mark's situation. For example, the answer to Jesus' first question uses terms of identification available in the Palestine of Jesus' earthly lifetime, but the answer to the second question and the teachings beginning in v. 34 employ the language of the early church ("the Christ," "take up his cross," "the gospel's"). In Perrin's judgment, "Jesus" in this story represents the risen Lord, "Peter" represents certain fallible believers, and "the multitude" represents

the entire membership of the church (Perrin 1969, 41–42). This double aspect of the New Testament materials (as handing on the tradition about Jesus
on the one hand, but on the other hand of doing so in such fashion as to proclaim the Lord in relation to the situation and needs of the church setting in
which that proclamation is being presented) is a basic point of emphasis in
both form criticism and redaction criticism.

Building upon previous form-critical studies, Perrin argues that this passage can be seen to include instances of three distinct kinds of redactional
work. In Mark 8:36–37 previously independent sayings have been brought
together; in 8:38 there is a modification of a saying from the form in which it
had come to Mark in the tradition; and in 9:1, the climactic promise of the
passage, there is a new saying created by the evangelist from materials already present in the traditions—both of the church and of Jewish apocalyptic (ibid., 44–51). That such redactional work is part of a careful editorial
development is shown, argues Perrin, by the repeated pattern of prediction,
misunderstanding, and teaching. He points out that the section of material
in Mark from 8:27 to 10:52 that introduces the Passion narrative is held
together by three geographical references: (1) "the villages of Caesarea
Philippi" (8:27), that is, north of Galilee; (2) a report of passing through Galilee in 9:30; and (3) the journey to Judea and beyond the Jordan (10:1), that
is, moving toward Jerusalem. In each of these three contexts there is a prediction of the Passion (8:31; 9:31; 10:33–34). The first of these is followed by
the dispute between Jesus and Peter and then by the teaching about disciple-
ship (8:32–37). The second is followed by the misunderstanding concerning
greatness and Jesus' teaching thereon (9:33–37). The third Passion prediction is followed immediately by the account of James's and John's misunderstanding concerning participation in Jesus' glory and Jesus' teaching on
that subject (10:35–45). There is, then, a very carefully constructed editorial
pattern building dramatically toward the Passion narrative (Perrin 1969, 45).

In looking at the Caesarea Philippi incident as presented by Mark, Perrin
notes that it places much emphasis upon persecution and suffering. This indicates, he argues, that Mark was writing for a situation in which Christians
were subject to persecution precisely for being Christians, and that Mark was
seeking to strengthen them for this persecution by relating it retrospectively
to Jesus' sufferings and prospectively to their final destiny. Here again, the
argument is that the evangelist was not merely reporting historical events,
but was interpreting the gospel tradition specifically in terms of the needs of
his own situation in the early church (ibid., 51–52).

In turning to the question of the place of this passage in Mark's Gospel as a
whole, Perrin is concerned with emphasizing that this decisive turning point

of the Gospel is particularly focused upon Christology, the question of the meaning of the affirmation that Jesus is the Christ. He points out that this title, "Christ," so familiar in the early church, is used only seven times in Mark. Examination of these uses (1:1; 8:29; 9:41; 12:35; 13:21; 14:61; 15:32) reveals that in only one of them (8:29) "is Jesus formally acknowledged as the Messiah of Jewish expectation and the Christ of Christian worship" (Perrin 1969, 54). This indicates a very special focus upon Christology in this account of the Caesarea Philippi incident.

Perrin sees further indication of this christological focus in the observation that this account marks a double transition in Mark's depiction of the disciples' understanding of Jesus. Throughout Mark's Gospel up to this point the disciples appear to be incapable of discerning who Jesus is, showing much less insight than persons lacking their special relationship to him. At Caesarea Philippi the disciples, represented by Peter, change from lack of understanding to misunderstanding. Peter calls him "the Christ," but his rejection of Jesus' prediction of suffering, death, and resurrection, and Jesus' strong condemnation thereof ("Get behind me, Satan! For you are not on the side of God, but of men") indicate that this represents a serious misunderstanding of Jesus' messiahship.

Perrin points out that there was a widespread basis for misunderstanding the affirmation of Jesus as the Christ in the early church because the idea of "divine men" (also called "sons of God"), men who employed miraculous powers to show their divinity, was a familiar one in the Greek world. Mark's Gospel actually presents Jesus in just such fashion right up to the Caesarea Philippi incident. The depiction invites the identification of Jesus in terms of this concept of a "divine man," and the suggestion is that this is what Peter confessed when he called Jesus "Christ." Thus when Jesus predicted suffering as inherent in his Christhood, Peter rebuked him, and Jesus in turn repudiated Peter's misinterpretation.

This focus of Mark's Gospel upon a false interpretation of Jesus as the Christ is further underlined by the second aspect of the change in the disciples' attitude toward Jesus. In addition to the shift from lack of understanding to misunderstanding, there is following Caesarea Philippi the development of rejection of Jesus by the disciples: betrayal by Judas, failure of the inner circle in Gethsemane, denial by Peter.

In light of these several indications of the carefully schematized structure of Mark's Gospel and its critical christological focus in the Caesarea Philippi incident, Perrin argues that Mark was not in fact concerned here with reporting an instance of the misunderstanding of Jesus on the part of Peter, but was rather concerned with mounting an attack upon an erroneous Christology that was powerfully at work in the church of Mark's time. "Peter" and "the disciples" embody this misunderstanding in the church, and Mark's re-presentation of the tradition repudiates the "divine man" interpretation of Jesus' messiahship and proclaims a Suffering Servant Christology (ibid., 56). The importance of the basic difference between these two Christologies in a situation in which the members of the church are facing persecution should be evident.

The discernment of the distinctiveness of the redactional work in Matthew and Luke is somewhat easier, as indicated above, due to the fact that we have before us in Mark one of their principal sources and can therefore see just how they adapt the material to their situations.

When one sets the Matthean version of the Caesarea Philippi incident (Matt. 16:13–23) next to the account in Mark 8, the most striking difference is the insertion of a paragraph in Matthew that completely changes the focus of the report. Immediately following Peter's confession of Jesus as the Christ, Matthew's version adds,

> And Jesus answered him, "Blessed are you, Simon Bar-Jona! For flesh and blood has not revealed this to you, but my Father who is in heaven. And I tell you, you are Peter, and on this rock I will build my church, and the powers of death shall not prevail against it. I will give you the keys of the kingdom of heaven, and whatever you bind on earth shall be bound in heaven, and whatever you loose on earth shall be loosed in heaven." (16:17–19, RSV)

Here there is no possibility that Peter's confession represents a christological misunderstanding (as in Mark), for it is the result of a special divine revelation. Perrin argues that the use of the incident in the two Gospels is quite different, for whereas it focuses upon Christology in Mark, here in Matthew it is concerned primarily with the founding of the church (Perrin 1969, 58). This observation is entirely in keeping with the common recognition that Matthew's Gospel as a whole deals with questions about the church as these confronted Christian congregations late in the first century. The observation that Matthew "added" these verses is not taken to mean that he "invented" them. One indication that these verses were a unit of tradition received by Matthew (in spite of their absence from both Mark and Luke) is the conflict between one of their affirmations and teachings elsewhere in Matthew. One of the implications of v. 19 (". . . and whatever you bind on earth shall be bound in heaven, . . .") is that salvation is guaranteed to those who are members of the church in good standing. Perrin judges that in such passages as Matt. 13:26–30 and 13:47–50 the First Gospel opposes this view of the church (ibid., 59).

The addition of vv. 17–19, while the most obvious, is not the only change made by Matthew in his account of the Caesarea Philippi incident. At the outset the question "Who do men say that I am?" (Mark 8:27) has become "Who do men say that the Son of man is?" (Matt. 16:13). In Mark's version of this incident the first reference to the title "Son of man" appears after Peter's confession when Jesus begins his teaching on his forthcoming suffering. Matthew's moving of it to the question is most peculiar, for it puts the answer into the question, "Son of man" being one of the most familiar christological titles in the early church. Perrin argues that this shows that Matthew was not interested in a realistic question initiating a christological discussion (as in Mark), but is here again focusing upon the founding of the church and emphasizing with this title the authority of the founder (Perrin 1969, 60–61).

Another indication of the evangelist's adaptation of the tradition for the setting for which he is composing his Gospel is Matthew's addition of the words "the Son of the living God" to Peter's confession. Perrin points out that the title "Son of God" was not a part of the vocabulary of the situation of Jesus' earthly ministry, but it was the common confession in the early church. Matthew is speaking to his own situation in its language. He is not merely reporting, but interpreting (ibid., 61).

The evidence of the creative work of the redactor is also discernible in Luke's treatment of the Caesarea Philippi incident. Most obvious here is that Luke's version completely omits the dispute between Jesus and Peter. Perrin contends that whereas this passage is central to the christological point in Mark, Luke is not concerned with Christology here. His own interest is indicated by "a series of subtle touches" such as his insertion of the word "daily" (Luke 9:23, RSV—"If any man would come after me, let him deny himself and take up his cross daily and follow me"). He also omits from Mark's version the phrase "in this adulterous and sinful generation" (Mark 8:38; Luke 9:26), and the words "come with power" in the concluding promise (Mark 9:1; Luke 9:27). Taken together, such apparently minor emendations basically alter the tone of the Markan passage specifically in terms of the teaching about the eschaton (the last judgment). "The Marcan note of urgency in the face of a specific persecution preceding an imminent eschaton has become a challenge for a continual witnessing over an indefinite period of time" (Perrin 1969, 63). Such a change is characteristic of a major Lukan theme according to Hans Conzelmann's pioneering redaction-critical studies of Luke in his *Theology of St. Luke.*

Thus redaction criticism seeks to show that the Synoptic evangelists play a far more important role in the history of Christian tradition than that of mere recorders and repeaters of past events or traditions. Each of them is an author and theologian interpreting the tradition in relation to the situation and needs of the Christian community in his own time and place, as illustrated by Perrin's argument that each represents the tradition concerning the incident at Caesarea Philippi in the context of a different theological concern: Mark—christological; Matthew—ecclesiological; Luke—eschatological.

Certainly Perrin's case has not been set forth here in sufficient detail to make possible judgments as to its persuasiveness. This sketch is included here only for the purpose of illustrating the nature of redaction criticism. Perrin's own presentation is offered as but an illustration, and calls for the careful consideration of several other studies. Redaction-critical studies include many inferences and judgments of probability. Each contribution is set forth for the critical scrutiny of other biblical scholars, and the process of ongoing debate and discussion about each point is a crucial element in determining the most probable interpretations. Redaction criticism is still in its early stages, and it would be premature to speak of its assured results in specific interpretations. On the other hand, it does seem fair to say that the work of the redaction critics has convincingly demonstrated that the evangelists to whom we owe the composition of the Synoptic Gospels were creative theologians, not merely compilers and editors, and that their theological work must be taken into account when one seeks to interpret their Gospels.

The Freedom of the Evangelists
Toward the Tradition

It should be noted that to speak of these evangelists as authors and to emphasize their contributions to Christian tradition is not to foreclose such questions as the place of revelation and the role of inspiration in the formation of the Gospels. It is sometimes suggested that form criticism and redaction criticism entail the judgment that various elements in the Gospels have been "invented" by the evangelists or by their predecessors in the development of the tradition. If the term "invented" is taken to mean that they arbitrarily introduced their own ideas and preferences into the tradition, then that is *not* the understanding required by or usually employed in form and redaction criticism. Perrin, for example, warns against this misunderstanding.

> We have spoken of Mark throughout as a self-conscious—one might even say cold-blooded!—editor, redactor, and author. We should perhaps stress the obvious fact that this is simply a scholarly convenience as we discuss what he did, and it is not meant to prejudge any questions with regard to inspiration, sense of having "the mind of the Lord," view of the tradition and its relationship to Jesus, etc. But before any such questions can be discussed, it is essential to be clear as to what Mark in fact did, and to determine that is, in part, the purpose of redaction criticism. (Ibid., 51n)

The problem concerning the findings of form and redaction criticism that changes took place in the development of the tradition and that the evangelists manifested considerable freedom in their adaptations of the traditions coming to them arises largely from the later idea that "inspiration" means a guaranteed preservation of exact details and from the modern historical concern with objective facts. As to the latter, Perrin, for example, has pointed out that

> we must strenuously avoid the assumption that the ancient world thought as the modern western world thinks. This is such a truism that one is almost ashamed to pen the words, and yet it remains a fact that, in a great deal of the more conservative biblical scholarship, it does seem to be assumed that the appeal to factual accuracy would be as valid and important a factor in the case of ancient Near Eastern religious texts as it would be in a modern western court of law or in a somewhat literally-minded western congregation. Against this it can only be stated that this is simply not the case. No ancient texts reflect the attitudes characteristic of the modern western world, and some of the difficulties to be seen in texts about Jesus could be matched by difficulties to be seen in texts about Pythagoras or Socrates. (Perrin 1967, 26)

It is, however, not only that they did not share our modern sense of historical accuracy, but also that we fail usually to take into account their sense of the living Lord. The conclusion of modern New Testament criticism that we are not given in the Gospels modern objective historical reporting of the life and teachings of Jesus is based upon what has been learned about the faith of the early Christian community. As Günther Bornkamm has put it,

> Faith in Jesus Christ, the Crucified and Resurrected, is by no means a later stratum of the tradition, but its very foundation, and the place from which it sprang and grew and from which alone it is intelligible. From this faith in Jesus, the Crucified and Exalted, both characteristics of the primitive Christian tradition can be understood—the obvious pains taken to preserve the tradition about Jesus conscientiously and faithfully but at the same time the peculiar freedom with which this tradition is presented in detail. The evangelists do not hark back to some kind of church archives when they pass on the words and deeds of Jesus, but they draw them from the kerygma [the proclamation] of the Church and serve this kerygma. Because Jesus is not a figure of the past and thus is no museum piece, there can be no "archives" for the primitive Christian tradition about him, in which he is kept. This insight into the nature of the tradition about Jesus is confirmed in detail again and again. (Bornkamm, Barth, and Held 1963, 52–53)

For the early church, the risen Lord who now speaks through prophets and evangelists is identified with the earthly Jesus. Hence Marxsen can say concerning a particular passage, "Here as elsewhere, Mark does not give thought to utterances of the historical Jesus. It is rather the Risen Lord who speaks—through the evangelist" (Marxsen 1969, 170). Perrin points out the evidences of this same understanding in the letters of Paul, and notes concerning the passage of the Lord's Supper in 1 Corinthians 11,

> Precisely because for him risen Lord and earthly Jesus are one and the same person, it would be a matter of complete indifference to him whether all, some, *or none*, of the words ascribed to the "Lord Jesus" of the paranese had, in fact, been spoken by the earthly Jesus to his disciples at an actual Passover, since they were being spoken by the risen Lord to his Church at the Eucharist. (Perrin 1967, 27)

When these differences between modern assumptions and those of the early church are taken into account, it becomes possible for us to understand the freedom of the evangelists in the composing of the Gospels. At the same time, however, we are reminded that in dealing with the Gospels we are not dealing with modern biography and historiography. These documents are part of the proclamation of the early church, and several stages of the process of Christian theological interpretation are to be detected in them and behind them.

Historical-Critical Problems Regarding Our Knowledge of Paul's Life and Teachings

The foregoing sketches of the development of biblical criticism have dealt briefly with the Pentateuch and thereafter focused entirely upon the Synoptic Gospels. Accordingly they represent a very incomplete indication of the scope of the problems that have confronted biblical scholarship. There are several other kinds of literature among the books of the Bible, and each kind presents the interpreter with special problems.

Consider the situation regarding Paul and his teaching. Here the circumstances are certainly very different from those involving our knowledge of the life and teachings of Jesus. In this case we have several letters written by Paul himself. In addition there is the extensive treatment of his life and teaching in the Book of Acts.

It is true that more is known of Paul than of any other person in primitive Christianity, but it remains the case that this knowledge is very incomplete. The information provided in Acts, far from offering a simple supplement to what may be learned from the letters, constitutes another set of problems, for it contains significant differences from the letters both as to the activities and the teachings of Paul.

The traditional belief that Acts provides "eyewitness" information and may therefore be counted upon to be factually accurate is subject to doubt on several grounds. Modern scholarship confirms that the Book of Acts was written by the author of the Gospel according to Luke and that these two books were written as one continuous "history," but it finds many reasons for doubting that that author was Luke, the companion of Paul. The earliest evidence of the tradition that Luke, the physician and the friend of Paul, was the author comes from late in the second century (Fitzmyer 1981, 35–53).

Even if one gives credence to the belief in Luke's authorship, however, the evidence of the document itself—especially when compared with Paul's letters—makes it clear that "Luke" was not a modern historian concerned with reporting the objective facts. The common practices of ancient reporting of historical events allowed far more liberty for embellishment and adaptation than do today's concepts of history. Critical study of Acts has been able to show, for example, that it is highly probable that the many speeches recorded in Acts are compositions of "Luke," not the words of the apostles. One of the indications of this is the significant difference to be seen between Paul's teaching in these speeches and in his letters.

The Book of Acts was written some forty years after Paul's letters—though it shows no awareness of those letters, which evidently had not yet been collected and circulated. Forty years does not seem very long to us as we consider it nineteen centuries later, but the scholars have found that it entailed important changes in the situation of the Christian community. The issues causing conflict in the churches at the time of the writing of Acts were different from those Paul addressed in his letters, and correspondingly, the understanding of Paul's teachings and of Christian faith itself had been modified. No careful scholar concludes from this that there are no trustworthy accounts in the Book of Acts, but they do conclude that the utmost caution must be exercised in judging where such trustworthiness is to be found, and they also insist that Acts must take second place to Paul's letters as a source for knowledge of the life and teaching of Paul.

The study of the letters involves another range of critical problems. For example, how many of the fourteen books of the New Testament traditionally identified as letters of Paul may be safely judged to be his? Careful examination has convincingly shown that Hebrews, 1 and 2 Timothy, and Titus cannot have been written by Paul, and many scholars are persuaded that Ephesians, Colossians, and 2 Thessalonians must also be designated as Deutero-Pauline (that is, written by someone else in the tradition of Pauline teaching). This leaves seven letters (Romans, 1 and 2 Corinthians, Galatians, Philippians, 1 Thessalonians, and Philemon) that are widely agreed upon as genuinely Pauline (Bornkamm 1971, 241–43). The factors involved in these judgments (and the arguments and counterarguments) are quite complex. They include differences in language, style, and theological teaching, and indications of later circumstances, such as the assumption of the postapostolic church order evident in 1 and 2 Timothy and Titus.

The complexity of these issues can be illustrated by a glance at the continuing debate concerning the authorship of 2 Thessalonians. Among the letters whose Pauline authorship has been questioned, there is more defense of Paul's writing of this than of any of the others. Doubts have, however, been raised on several grounds.

To begin with, a general problem arises in the fact that there is a distinct contrast in the problems dealt with in the two letters. First Thessalonians seeks to reassure persons who are distressed by the fact that some have died before the final judgment. The problem is the delay of the end. Second Thessalonians seeks rather to refute the teaching that the end has already come, and insists that it has not yet come. If Paul wrote both, how has so marked a change taken place in the church at Thessalonica? Has a long period of time intervened? Careful comparison of the two letters shows strong similarities in terms and wording that suggest either that Paul wrote the second so soon after the first that he had it still firmly in mind, or that the first letter was used by someone else in the writing of the second (Marxsen 1970, 40–41). Here the case for Paul's authorship rules out the theory of a long gap to account for the changed situation. To solve the problem without the conclusion of non-Pauline authorship others have suggested: (1) that Paul wrote to two different groups within the congregation at Thessalonica; (2) that 2 Thessalonians was written first; and (3) that 2 Thessalonians was really addressed to Philippi. Each of these suggestions provides some help for the problem, but also raises other difficulties (ibid., 41–42).

Further difficulties are posed by the fact that alongside the very great linguistic and stylistic similarities between the two letters there are marked theological contrasts. Most often mentioned is the difference in teachings concerning the end. First Thessalonians teaches that it is very near. Second Thessalonians proclaims a considerable delay in its coming, which it sets forth in an apocalyptic outline of events quite unlike anything appearing elsewhere in Paul's letters (2 Thess. 2:3–12). Other differences in teaching that suggest 2 Thessalonians comes from a later period than Paul's letters have been summarized by R. H. Fuller as follows:

> There is a different view of the last judgment. In Paul every man, pagan and Christian alike, will be judged according to his works (pagans: Rom 2:6–11; Christians: Rom 14:10–12; I Cor 4:4f; 2 Cor 5:10). In Paul only false teachers will be judged as such (Gal 5:10; 2 Cor 11:15). In 2 Thess, on the other hand, the last judgment relates to two general classes, the persecuted church and its persecutors. At the last judgment there will be a reversal of fates: the persecutors will have tribulation and the persecuted relief (2 Thess 1:5ff; cf. Rev 16:6f, 19:2). Finally Braun notes a tendency, characteristic of the post-Pauline generation, to transfer attributes, functions, etc., from God to Christ, e.g. 2 Thess 2:16, 3:5 compared with 1 Thess 3:11f. (Fuller 1966, 58)

These theological differences suggest, in H. Braun's view, that 2 Thessalonians was written in the postapostolic age. This would readily account for the markedly different situation being addressed, and it would see the peculiar linguistic dependence as resulting from the use of Paul's letter as a model.

New Testament scholars differ concerning the weight of these arguments, and the question of the authorship of 2 Thessalonians remains a matter of doubt and debate. Does it really matter? Robert M. Grant suggests that it does not, commenting, "The function of historical analysis is not to show why a document should not be regarded as genuine but to accept it and try to understand its situation" (Grant 1963, 179). This is a very peculiar remark, for the issues involved in this discussion are directly concerned with the attempt to understand the situation of the letter. Judgments about both the authorship and the date will affect the interpreter's understanding of that situation and therefore of the letter, and if one judges that Paul is the author that will affect the interpretation of Paul's other letters.

Certainly the discussion of these issues is not the same as dealing with the question of the meaning of these texts for us, but it is to deal with matters that are relevant thereto. The determination of the historical setting is important for understanding the author's meaning. If we misconstrue the problems to which he speaks, we are likely to misunderstand what he affirms also.

The problem of ascertaining the historical circumstances in which a letter was written arises differently in relation to the Corinthian correspondence. Here it is not a question whether or not Paul is the author (except in relation to 2 Cor. 6:14—7:1), but how many different letters and different situations are represented in the materials we have in 2 Corinthians. The most obvious break is between chapters 9 and 10. The conciliatory tone of the earlier chapters is in sharp contrast to the attack upon persons who question the legitimacy of Paul's apostleship in chapters 10—13. Two very different situations are reflected. Contrasts do not end there, however. For example, chapters 8 and 9 both deal with the subject of the collection for Jerusalem, but they do so very differently, reflecting contrasting situations. Such factors have led many scholars to judge that the present 2 Corinthians includes fragments from several letters. Marxsen, for example, proposes the following list:

> a conciliatory letter: i. 3–ii. 13 and vii. 5–16;
> an apologia: ii. 14–vi. 13 and vii. 2–4;
> a violent attack: x–xiii;
> two letters concerning the collection: viii and ix;
> an apocalyptic exhortation (probably non-Pauline): vi. 14–vii. 1. (Marxsen 1970, 79)

Other scholars propose different interpretations of the breaks and contrasts in 2 Corinthians, but in each case must use every tool available to the interpreter to attempt to reconstruct the relations between Paul and the Corinthian congregation reflected in the various parts of our present letter.

It should be evident, even from these brief indications, that historical-critical problems abound as much for the interpreter of Paul's letters as they do for the student of the Synoptic Gospels. In fact, anyone who will take the trouble to examine any reputable modern introduction to the books of the Bible will find this to be true throughout the several kinds of literature that make up the Christian Scriptures (e.g., Crenshaw 1986; Eissfeldt 1965; Fuller 1966; Grant 1963).

The Canon of the New Testament

Concerning the canon of the New Testament, the list of books that constitute the distinctively Christian Scriptures, there has long been almost complete agreement. That does not mean, however, that current Christian scholarship has been without serious problems in this area of historical-critical scholarship.

The long-cherished tradition that the twenty-seven books of the New Testament were designated toward the end of the first century by John, the son of Zebedee, was shown to be false by the application of the methods of modern historical research, which established that some of those books were written later. Nineteenth-century scholarship concluded that most of the New Testament canon was established by about the end of the second century. This view prevailed until the 1970s when further study of the evidence and the arguments showed it more probable that this core of the New Testament had not achieved canonical status until the fourth century. The first known list that agrees completely with the twenty-seven books that came finally to constitute the New Testament canon was in a letter of Athanasius, bishop of Alexandria, in the year 367. Disagreements concerning the inclusion or exclusion of certain books continued long thereafter, however. The Council of Constantinople in 692, for example, approved a list including *1* and *2 Clement* and excluding Revelation (Sundberg 1976, 140).

The first generations of Christians evidently felt no need for a "New Testament." They assumed the authority of the Hebrew Scriptures, and they understood themselves to be under the guidance of the risen Lord. They also expected the final judgment to bring this world to an end very soon, so the apostles' memories of the Lord seemed sufficient.

The central factor in all of this was Jesus Christ. Therefore the Hebrew Scriptures did not have the same meaning for the Christians as they did for the Jews. Their authority was assumed, but their meaning was in their pointing to Christ, and not as a set of norms for daily life. Thus, "Early Christianity is positively not to be regarded as a 'religion of the book'; it is the religion of the Spirit and of the living Christ" (Campenhausen 1968, 62–63).

A. C. Sundberg notes that in view of these several considerations it is surprising that the Gospels were written, and he reports that Papias, the first we know of to make written mention of any Gospel, writing about 130, defended the Gospel of Mark but showed a clear preference for the oral tradition about Jesus (Sundberg 1976, 137).

The first evidence we have of an appeal to the authority of the Gospels as equivalent to that of the Hebrew Scriptures is in the writing of Justin Martyr (d. ca. 165). It is not clear, however, whether Justin knew a four-Gospel canon, and this was a period during which other gospels (since excluded from our canon) were being used among the churches. Justin did not accord scriptural status to any other Christian writings. Indeed, he did not even quote Paul's letters.

By the end of the second century there is much more evidence of attribution of scriptural authority to Christian writings, though there continues to be disagreement among scholars concerning the extent to which one may properly speak of a New Testament canon at that time. Sundberg has pointed out that the influential Christian teachers of the second century treated such writings as *1 Clement,* the *Letters* of Ignatius, the *Epistle of Barnabas, The Shepherd of Hermas,* and Polycarp's writings as having the same authority they attributed to the writings that were to become the official Christian Scriptures (Sundberg 1975, 363–64). And R. P. C. Hanson has shown that a New Testament canon, as we understand that term, not only was not present in Clement of Alexandria, but is also not to be found in his great successor, Origen (in the middle of the third century) (Hanson 1954, 143).

No doubt the arguments about the extent to which one may speak of a firm sense of New Testament canon before the fourth century will continue. What is evident in the midst of the arguments is that the development of our New Testament list was a very gradual and a very human one. The reasons for inclusion and exclusion are more enlightening than the dates of the decisions.

The doctrine that there are four and only four authoritative Gospels comes from Irenaeus, late in the second century. His reason for limiting the number of Gospels to four is that this is the very nature of things, there being four zones of the world, four principal winds, and so forth (Irenaeus, 3.11.8,i). It has been argued that this was not Irenaeus's reason for the limit of four, but only an indication of its appropriateness, for, as F. S. Gutjahr argued, "The four-fold Gospel is simply an historic fact enshrined in the tradition of the Church, . . ." (Lawson 1948, 44). That clearly was not "an historic fact" of

Irenaeus's time, however. Several other gospels were treated as authoritative by various Christian writers for some time after Irenaeus. Indeed, his argument was evoked by such use of another gospel. What one sees here is a desire to defend the originator of our fourfold Gospel doctrine against the recognition that he employed an argument that we could not today take seriously. But the fact that he did employ such an argument is but one of many indications that the persons who established the limits of the Christian canon lived in times and with assumptions and information very different from our own, and the arguments that influenced them in the determinations we inherit are not generally arguments with which we can concur.

Far more important in the granting of authority to writings was the judgment as to their *apostolicity*. If a teaching was judged to be from the apostles it had authority, but by the time the churches had developed the sense of need for authoritative Christian Scriptures, the bases for determining the authorship of early writings had become tenuous. The preponderance of modern New Testament scholarship is against the judgment that any of the canonical books as we now have them were written by any of the original disciples or their immediate followers. The apostle Paul is agreed to be the author of several of the New Testament letters, but modern scholars are largely agreed that he did not write all of the thirteen that the early church fathers attributed to him (the dubiousness of Paul's authorship of Hebrews was recognized very early).

The concept of "apostolicity" was not always so narrowly defined or applied by the church fathers as is often supposed. Irenaeus included under this term not only the original disciples and their immediate followers, but also the elders of the churches believed to have been founded by original apostles. In this way the concept of apostolicity was broadened and became entangled with judgments about orthodox content. This appears again in Origen's discussion of the Letter to the Hebrews. He acknowledged the uncertainty of its authorship, but commended its apostolic teaching and placed weight on its use among the churches (Hanson 1954, 141–42). Thus we find here what have been judged to be the three main criteria for determining canonicity in the early church: apostolic authorship, orthodox content, and common usage.

There is circularity in the application of these criteria. Common usage was related to what was believed to be from the apostles, and orthodox teaching is what one believed to be in accordance with the teachings of the apostles. But by the time the church set about deciding which writings should be regarded as authoritative, they had, in part, to appeal to the orthodoxy of a document's teaching as a basis for judging it to be "apostolic." In all this the human factors, with their historical and cultural relativities and their fallibilities, are clearly at work.

Some may protest that such a judgment ignores the most important factor regarding the canonical books, namely, that the reason they are canonical is that they are "inspired" writings. It is true that those in the early church who argued for the authoritative status of particular writings believed those writings to be inspired. It is also true that these same persons believed other writings to be inspired. Indeed, the doctrine that the canonical books and only the canonical books are "inspired" did not appear among Christians until after the first stages of the Protestant Reformation. In the early church the common view was that God's inspiration was at work throughout the church, and it was not, therefore, the criterion for including writings in the developing canon of the New Testament (Sundberg 1975).

In view of these many discoveries of modern historical research regarding the development of the list of New Testament Scriptures, it is hardly surprising that statements such as the following from Schubert Ogden on the New Testament canon are increasingly common among Christian scholars.

> It is the product indeed of the *experientia ecclesiae,* at least in the sense that it emerged only in the course of the church's continuing attempts to control the putative authorities that would control it in relation to the ultimate source of all authority in Christ himself. But, since "popes and councils can err," the canon that thus emerged from the early church's own experience and decisions is and must be open to revision. (Ogden 1976, 249)

Such statements should not be taken to mean that the authority of the traditional twenty-seven books is being denied or that there is any great movement under way to remove any of those books from or add others to the New Testament. Such suggestions are made from time to time, and one may note, for example, that even fairly conservative New Testament scholars see the *Gospel of Thomas* as one of our sources for knowledge of the early church's witness to Jesus Christ. It is more a matter of recognizing in principle that the selection of these twenty-seven books was a human and historical process that cannot reasonably be supposed to have set those writings apart from all other human writings as fundamentally different in kind.

One of the much-debated issues entailed with this recognition is the question of whether there must be a "canon within the canon," and, if so, what it should be. Representatives of the very conservative positions continue commonly to argue that the authority is equal throughout all parts of all twenty-seven books. It is easy to show, however, that any fairly consistent theology employs some kind of norm that places greater emphasis upon some writings and some teachings. This, in general, is what is meant by a "canon within the canon." If "canon" is understood to mean not simply the list of authoritative scriptures, but, as the term originally suggested, the "measure" or "standard" of Christian belief, and if it is acknowledged that there is a considerable variety of teaching found within the books that the churches gradually selected for the official list, it would seem to follow that there must be some kind of norm or standard for the use and interpretation of the canonical books. The recognition of the humanness of the selection of the books, together with the recognition of the humanness of the writing and editing of the books themselves, has made this problem inescapable for modern theology.

New Testament Textual Criticism

Another of the "firm foundations" of post-Reformation but premodern theology that has been shaken by modern biblical scholarship is the state of the text of the Greek New Testament. From the time of the Reformation until the mid-nineteenth century, the work of New Testament scholars was dependent upon published forms of the Greek New Testament based on a small number of relatively poor and late manuscripts. Throughout this period there was a *Textus Receptus*—a commonly received standard text. The designation itself came from an exaggerated advertiser's phrase used in the preface of a 1633 edition: ". . . the text which is now received by all, in which we give nothing changed or corrupted" (Metzger 1968, 106). The edition that became the Received Text in the English-speaking world was the third edition published by Stephanus in 1550, which in turn was based on the work of Erasmus (his 4th and 5th eds., 1527 and 1535 respectively) and the Complutensian Polyglot (1522). Bruce M. Metzger has pointed out that this tradition, though it is based on a "haphazard" collection of late manuscripts that include several passages unsupported in any known Greek text, is the main basis for the much-revered King James Version and all the other influential European Protestant translations made before 1881. That the reverence for this form of the New Testament text is still alive is witnessed by the title page of The Gideons International 1976 edition of the New Testament on which the following is to be found: "Translated out of the Original Tongues and with the Former Translations diligently compared—commonly known as the Authorized (King James) Version." No doubt there are many persons who take unwarranted comfort from these anachronistic words!

The situation today is very different from that in which the various editors of the *Textus Receptus* worked. Many many more and much older manuscripts are available, and the science of critical historiography has only developed between the two eras. It is no longer possible for a scholar to speak of a *Textus Receptus* except as a historical reference to that older, mistaken confidence. Textual critics are hard at work in continual efforts to improve the available critical editions of the Greek New Testament. That this should be so difficult a task is due first of all to the facts that there are more than five thousand manuscripts in many forms and languages, and that no two of these manuscripts agree completely with each other. One must hasten to add that the differences (of which there are tens of thousands) do not seriously affect the meaning of more than a very small portion of the New Testament. A recent indication of the amount that is in doubt is to be found in the several editions of the United Bible Societies' Greek New Testament (UBSGNT). The editors have included footnotes showing the manuscript sources for the exegetically important variants (in their judgment) for more than 1400 passages, and they have indicated their judgment of the degree of doubtfulness of their choices of the best texts in these cases. In round numbers, they judge 120 of these passages to be "virtually certain," 470 to entail only "some degree of doubt," 690 to involve "considerable doubt," and 150 to have a very high degree of doubt or no satisfactory reading. Thus, some 840 passages include textual problems serious enough to lead this committee of textual critics to conclude that we really cannot know what the best form of the text should be.

Such data suggest two questions: first, why do such uncertainties exist? and, second, how important are they? The answer to the first question lies in the history of the transmission of the texts. Because printing had not yet been invented, all Christian writings were written and copied laboriously by hand for the first fourteen centuries of the church's life. No original manuscript of any part of the New Testament is known to exist, and the oldest known copy of any portion of the New Testament is a papyrus fragment containing a few verses of the Fourth Gospel. Several scholars judge it to be from the first half of the second century. The earliest known copy of Luke is a papyrus dated between 175 and 225 c.e. There are some quotations of our New Testament books to be found in the writings of the church fathers in the second century. The earliest extant documents for larger portions of the New Testament come from the third and fourth centuries.

In most of the early manuscripts there is no division between words, and the use of punctuation was rare until the eighth century. The manuscript evidence shows that in the earlier stages of the process of copying the Christian writings generally less care was given to the control of accuracy than after the church was officially approved in the fourth century. Metzger notes that during these first stages when individual Christians were making copies of the manuscripts for themselves or their congregations, the rapid growth of Christianity led to a greater pressure for speed than for accurate reproduction. "Furthermore, in preparing translations or versions for persons who knew no

Greek, it occurred more than once (as Augustine complained) that 'anyone who happened to gain possession of a Greek manuscript and who imagined that he had some facility in both Latin and Greek, however slight it might be, dared to make a translation'" (ibid., 14).

Whether the copyist worked alone, with the eye passing back and forth from the model to the new copy, or with others, listening to someone's dictation from the manuscript being copied, it is hardly surprising that errors continually crept in, or that differences developed and became standard in different parts of the world, so that now it is possible to speak of text "families." Thus while certain kinds of copyists' errors are readily determinable and correction not difficult, other differences among the early manuscripts confront the textual critics with serious and sometimes insoluble problems.

In classifying the various kinds of causes of changes in the texts of the New Testament that they can readily identify, the textual critics have found not only accidental changes due to faulty eyesight, faulty hearing, and so forth, but also *intentional changes*. These include correcting the text (in the copyist's judgment) because of disagreement with another text, historical or geographical information, addition of details, and even theological points. An illustration of such a theological change is to be found in most of the Greek manuscripts of Luke 23:32, where the sentence, "And also other criminals, two, were led away with him to be crucified," has been changed to, "And also two others, criminals, were led away with him to be crucified" (UBS trans., ibid., 202). There was evidently a concern to remove the implication that Jesus was a criminal. Another example given by Metzger is Mark 13:32 and Matt. 24:36, where some scribes omitted "nor the Son" from the statement, "But of that day and hour no one knows, not even the angels of heaven, nor the Son, but the Father only."

After giving such illustrations, Metzger hastens to add,

> Lest the foregoing examples of alterations should give the impression that scribes were altogether wilful and capricious in transmitting ancient copies of the New Testament, it ought to be noted that other evidence points to the careful and painstaking work on the part of many faithful copyists. There are, for example, instances of difficult readings which have been transmitted with scrupulous fidelity. (Ibid., 206)

For most of the New Testament, then, the textual critics have been able to determine what is very probably the oldest form of the text. There are, on the other hand, hundreds of passages that remain steeped in uncertainty. It is in relation to these passages that the disagreements among the textual critics have become apparent. These disagreements include not only the judgments of which is the best reading in each case, but even the methods that should be employed to decide which form of the text should be preferred. It is possible that some of the uncertainties will be resolved by further discoveries of ancient manuscripts, but it cannot reasonably be expected that all such questions will be answered; they are rooted in the manuscripts themselves and the nature and history of their transmission. Inevitably some uncertainties will remain.

How important are these continuing textual uncertainties? This question may be focused upon particular texts or upon New Testament textual problems as a whole. A few illustrations will be useful for both.

The last half of John 7:39 is given in seven different forms in the manuscripts. The editors of the UBSGNT judge that the briefest of these is virtually certain as the original reading. In English it would be translated, "for as yet the Spirit was not, because Jesus was not yet glorified" (ibid., 225). The problem with this text is theological—it might well be taken to mean that the Spirit did not exist at that time. Many of the later manuscripts include "clarifications" of this point. Interestingly, our recent translations such as the RSV (Revised Standard Version) and the NEB (New English Bible) follow some of the later manuscripts, and instead of "for as yet the Spirit was not," they give "for as yet the Spirit had not been given" (RSV), etc. This is even true of the American Bible Society's Today's English Version (TEV), which is published specifically as a translation of the UBSGNT, but in this case does not follow the Greek text. Neither the RSV nor the NEB nor the TEV gives any indication that the best text is not being followed. In this case we do not have an uncertainty among the text critics regarding what is most probably the original form of the text, but a fear shared by ancient scribes and modern translators that readers will not be able to cope with the original text!

A better illustration of an uncertain text is to be found in Acts 20:28. The verse, as translated in some early editions of the RSV, reads, "Take heed to yourselves and to all the flock, in which the Holy Spirit has made you guardians, to feed the church of the Lord which he obtained with his own blood." As the RSV indicates in a footnote, "Other ancient authorities read *of God*" rather than "of the Lord." As Metzger explains, there are seven different readings for this point in the ancient manuscripts (ibid., 234). Of these, however, only the two indicated by the RSV are well attested in the oldest manuscripts. But they are equally well attested, so the textual critics have to make their judgments concerning which is more likely to be the original reading on the basis of "internal probabilities." That is, it cannot be decided on the basis of the oldest and best manuscripts, so attention is turned to the probabilities as to which of the two forms ("of God," "of the Lord") would more likely have been changed to the other.

While there are several factors that may be taken into account here, it seems that the central problem is that if the text reads "the church of God," the following clause might be taken to imply that God has blood. Thus many argue that it is more likely that "of God" would have been changed to "of the Lord" to remove this suggestion than that the reverse change would have been made, there being no reason for such a change. It has also been suggested that the final clause could mean "with the blood of his Own" instead of "with his own blood." Both the RSV and the NEB choose "of the Lord" and indicate these alternatives in footnotes. The editors of the UBSGNT chose "of God," but indicated that there is considerable doubt. The TEV here followed their Greek text and used "of God," but then departed considerably from the Greek of the final clause, dropping out any use of the term "blood" and giving instead, "which he made his own through the death of his Son." The footnote indicating alternative possibilities does not indicate that the Greek here speaks of "blood."

What one finds here, then, is not only an illustration of an uncertainty about the exact reading of the original Greek text which may entail a theological problem, but also an illustration of the fact that the vast majority of readers are at the mercy of both ancient scribes and modern translators and editors.

These illustrations of uncertainties about particular texts show that if great weight is to be placed on individual texts, at the very least careful attention must be paid to the helps offered the nonspecialist by the textual critics. Certainly some of the uncertain texts entail theological issues. More important, however, is the dubiousness of placing great weight on particular texts rather than upon the biblical witnesses dealt with (insofar as possible) as a whole.

When one asks how important the continuing textual uncertainties are for the New Testament as a whole, the answer depends upon one's point of view. For those who accept the judgment that the texts themselves show the Scriptures to be human and historical writings that therefore manifest historical and cultural relativities, prejudices, and fallibilities, the uncertain state of some texts is simply another aspect of a general situation. Those persons will not attempt to prove either historical or theological points on the basis of individual texts. If, however, the attempt is made to maintain the post-Reformation doctrine of the verbal inerrancy of the Scriptures, it will be necessary to appeal to the supposed perfection of unrecoverable manuscripts —a meaningless escape from the manifest problems. To maintain some semblance of reasonableness, close attention should be paid to the labors of textual critics in order to avoid dogmatic use of doubtful texts. Those who take the verbal-inerrancy viewpoint are, however, not commonly inclined to follow the text critics' methods for determining the "best reading," usually determining the choice on dogmatic grounds instead. That is, "such and such must be the correct text because my orthodoxy requires it."

THE GENERAL IMPACT OF HISTORICAL-CRITICAL BIBLICAL SCHOLARSHIP

One might be tempted to suppose that the continuing debates among biblical scholars show this kind of study to be more a source of confusion and frustration than of enlightenment. Such a conclusion would overlook at least three important considerations. First, such debates are the way in which scholars in this and other fields test the persuasiveness of their hypotheses, discover where they have been misled by their own predilections, and learn of relevant considerations they have overlooked. Second, agreement has been reached by most scholars on many important issues through this process. Third, underlying all of the many disagreements among the historical-critical biblical scholars there is a basic agreement that is of the greatest importance for Christian theology, the recognition that the Bible is composed of "historical" documents.

The Historical Nature of the Scriptures

This recognition has been made possible by the gradually increasing freedom during the past three centuries to examine the books of the Bible without the constraint of prior dogmatic conclusions about their nature. This constraint was internal as well as external, for the force of cultural conditioning built upon many centuries of religious conviction made it extremely difficult for the scholars themselves to "see" the Scriptures other than through glasses tinted by dogma. Gradually, however, accumulating studies have shown that the Bible is not a body of *timeless* truths. Even today one will often hear the expression, "the Bible says, . . ." As usually employed, this phrase suggests that the materials in the Bible are somehow equally and *directly* relevant to this and every other time and situation. What has become increasingly clear, however, is that the biblical writings cannot be understood without regard to the settings in which they came to expression. These writings spoke to their times in terms of the language, customs, beliefs, and problems of those times. Every book of the Bible manifests this historical and cultural relativity inescapably, and we must struggle to understand these relativities if we wish to understand what was being said then and there and what may be said to us here and now through such historical witnesses.

The Human Character of the Scriptures

That familiar phrase, "the Bible says, . . ." not only errs in its implication that the biblical writings are "timeless," but also in its assumption concerning the nature of the *unity* of the Bible. It is rooted in the belief that neither Moses, nor Isaiah, nor Paul, nor John is the real author of any book of the Bible, because God is the true author of all of them. It would follow, then, that all of those books (and their parts) are in complete agreement with each other (except insofar as doctrines of "accommodation" have qualified the basic assumption in view of its manifest difficulties). The study of the books themselves, apart from the constraints of this dogma, has made it clear that there are significant differences in the teachings of the various biblical authors, such as between those of Paul and of the author of the pastoral epistles concerning such basic concepts as "faith" and "love." This is to affirm that a part of the "historical" character of the biblical writings is their "humanness." The limitations and the perspectives of the human authors are evident and important. We may well judge those witnesses to have been persons of faith, honesty, insight, and inspiration, but we can see that in their efforts to convey their convictions about the reality and the activity of God they were still human and not divine. They could only employ the language and the concepts that could be understood in their historical and cultural situations. Because of the implicit understanding of the world they shared as children of their times, they interpreted events and experiences in terms of assumptions that we need not and perhaps cannot share today. In their writings one may see evidence of the fallibility, the ignorance, and the prejudice that are part of every human life. The biblical writings are not infallible, and it is most unlikely that any of the biblical authors ever thought his or her writings were.

The False Dichotomy: Infallible or Worthless

Sometimes one will hear in response to statements such as these the judgment that if the Bible is not infallible, then it is untrustworthy and therefore worthless. This is an example of the fallacy of arguing by false dichotomy. That is, one suggests or assumes that there are only two possibilities and that therefore if one is false the other must be true. The assumption at work in the foregoing judgment is that either the Bible is infallible or else it is *entirely* fallible and therefore worthless. It is interesting to note that this same judgment is not made about any other writings. Why is it made, then, in the case of the Bible? The answer surely lies in the fact that one has found comfort and security in the dogma that the Bible is infallible and is therefore threatened by evidence that the dogma is false.

The same argument is present in the assumption that if the Bible is not infallible, then it is not "inspired." In this case one interpretation of the term "inspired" is presupposed when there are many possible interpretations of that term. The presupposition is again a matter of unexamined dogmatic commitment.

It is probable that most historical-critical biblical scholars believe the Bible to be "inspired," and it is clear that the vast majority of those scholars regard the biblical writings as being of the utmost significance for us at the same time that they point out the historical and cultural relativities and the human limitations they discover within them. There is no contradiction in this.

The Kerygmatic Purpose of the Scriptures

In addition to recognizing the historicity and the humanness of the documents, historical-critical research has also emphasized that the biblical writings are *kerygmatic*. The Greek word *kerygma* is usually translated "proclamation," and points to the evangelical concern of the authors and redactors, that is, their basic concern to evoke the response of faith to the affirmation of the grace of God. The recognition that the Gospels were seeking to proclaim the lordship of Jesus Christ rather than to report facts about Jesus of Nazareth has been one of the primary factors leading to the conclusion that we do not have any *direct* access to the kind of data that would provide the basis for an objective reporter's description of Jesus. The evangelists were not interested in such a depiction. They sought to confront their readers with the reality faith perceives, and while some persist in calling that "objective," it is not what historical research means by that term.

It is not only the Gospels, however, that are "kerygmatic" in this broad sense of the term. While the degree to which the evangelical intention is at work in the many different kinds of literature in the Bible certainly differs, it is, nevertheless, usually an important factor. The so-called historical books of the Old Testament, for example, were not written for the simple scholarly purpose of recording the factual events of the nation's life, but of interpreting that national life theologically for the sake of eliciting renewed faithfulness. From the standpoint of the modern concern with ascertaining "the facts," this theological-kerygmatic nature of the documents is seen as a deficiency, and it is not unusual for representatives of very conservative theological perspectives to see this characterization of the biblical writings as an attack on their "reliability." But scholars are not criticizing the books of the Bible. They are pointing out their nature in order that we may be less prone to ask of those writings what their authors had no intention of offering.

Here again, the popular notion of biblical infallibility is under attack, for that notion assumes that it was the purpose of the Scriptures to report "objective facts." The finding of historical-critical scholarship, however, is that the preoccupation with "objective facts" is a very modern concern simply not characteristic of the biblical writings.

Critical Questions for Modern Theology

These conclusions that the documents of the Bible are historical, human, and kerygmatic raise several important questions for theology. Ordinarily the Bible is seen as the primary source, norm, and authority for Christian theology. Those theologies that do not share this general affirmation of biblical primacy have the task of justifying their claim to be Christian theologies, for the term "Christian" derives from the affirmation that "Jesus is the Christ," and our only significant access to the community in which that affirmation began and to the person and the events that gave rise to it is the Bible. Therefore, a Christian theologian who accepts the general conclusions of historical-critical biblical scholarship and acknowledges the historical, human, and kerygmatic character of the Scriptures must assume the responsibility to answer such questions as: What is the nature of the biblical writings? Are some or all of them "inspired," and, if so, what does this term mean? What is meant by "revelation," and what is its relation to the books of the Bible? Should a distinction be made between "the Word of God" and the words of the Bible, and, if so, what is it? Just what does Christian theology need from the Bible—facts, information, doctrines, laws, evangelical witnessing, all of these things, or something else? When have we heard the essential biblical message? Is it when we have a "correct" intellectual grasp of its teachings? Is it when we respond in faith? Is it both of these? Or neither? How should we interpret the Scriptures in order to facilitate what is judged to be that "right hearing"? What kind of authority do biblical teachings have for us today? How are we to deal with differing biblical perspectives, emphases, theologies?

These are interrelated and overlapping questions, and they give rise to yet further questions. It is evident that there is no one simple "modern" theological alternative to the more traditional assumptions. For example, in relation to contemporary interpretations of "revelation," "modern" theologies agree in rejecting "propositional" revelation (the view that the very statements or propositions contained in the Scriptures are the content of God's special revelation), but vary widely in the positive interpretations they offer as to what is meant by "revelation."

These questions concerning revelation, inspiration, biblical authority, and biblical interpretation entangle each other and entail all of the other basic theological questions: our understanding of God, God's will, and how God acts. It should therefore be clear that the development of modern historical-critical biblical scholarship has confronted Christian theology with a most direct and basic challenge, and that no serious theological study in our time can proceed without grappling with this challenge.

WORKS CITED

Bornkamm, G.
  1971 [1969]   *Paul: Paulus.* Translated by D. M. Stalker. New York: Harper & Row.

Bornkamm, G., G. Barth, and H. J. Held
  1963   *Tradition and Interpretation in Matthew.* Translated by P. Scott. New Testament Library. Philadelphia: Westminster Press.

Bultmann, R.
  1963   *History of the Synoptic Tradition.* Translated from the 3d German ed. by J. Marsh. New York: Harper & Row.

Campenhausen, H. von
  1968   *The Formation of the Christian Bible.* Philadelphia: Fortress Press.

Conzelmann, H.
  1960   *Theology of St. Luke.* Translated by G. Buswell. New York: Harper & Row.

Crenshaw, J. L.
  1986   *Story and Faith: A Guide to the Old Testament.* New York: Macmillan Co.

Dibelius, M.
  1935   *From Tradition to Gospel.* Translated from the rev. 2d ed. by B. L. Woolf. New York: Charles Scribner's Sons.

Eissfeldt, O.
  1965   *The Old Testament: An Introduction.* Translated by Peter R. Ackroyd. New York: Harper & Row.

Filson, F. V.
  1971   "The Literary Relations Among the Gospels." In *The Interpreter's One-Volume Commentary on the Bible.* Edited by C. M. Laymon, 1129–35. Nashville: Abingdon Press.

Fitzmyer, J. A., S.J.
  1981   *The Gospel According to Luke (I–IX).* 2d ed. The Anchor Bible, vol. 28. Garden City, N.Y.: Doubleday & Co.

Fuller, R. H.
  1966   *A Critical Introduction to the New Testament.* London: Gerald Duckworth & Co.

Gideons International
  1976   *The New Testament of Our Lord and Savior Jesus Christ with*

Psalms and Proverbs. The Gideons International. 1976 ed. Philadelphia: National Publishing Co.

Grant, R. M.
1963   *A Historical Introduction to the New Testament*. New York: Harper & Row.

Hanson, R. P. C.
1954   *Origen's Doctrine of Tradition*. London: SPCK.

Irenaeus, Saint, bishop of Lyons
n.d.   *Five Books of S. Irenaeus against heresies*. Translated by J. Keble. London: A. D. Innes.

Lampe, G. W. H., and K. J. Woollcombe
1957   *Essays on Typology*. Naperville, Ill.: Alec R. Allenson.

Lawson, J.
1948   *The Biblical Theology of St. Irenaeus*. London: Epworth Press.

Marxsen, W.
1969   *Mark the Evangelist: Studies on the Redaction History of the Gospel*. Translated by J. Boyce, D. Juel, W. Poehlmann, with R. A. Harrisville. New York: Abingdon Press.

1970   *Introduction to the New Testament: An Approach to its Problems*. 3d ed. Translated by G. Buswell. Philadelphia: Fortress Press.

McKnight, E. V.
1969   *What Is Form Criticism?* Philadelphia: Fortress Press.

Metzger, B. M.
1968   *The Text of the New Testament: Its Transmission, Corruption, and Restoration*. 2d ed. New York: Oxford University Press.

Ogden, S. O.
1976   "The Authority of Scripture for Theology." *Interpretation* 30, no. 1 (1976): 242–61.

Perrin, N.
1967   *Rediscovering the Teaching of Jesus*. New York: Harper & Row.
1969   *What Is Redaction Criticism?* Philadelphia: Fortress Press.

Perry, A. M.
1951   "The Growth of the Gospels." In *The Interpreter's Bible*, vol. 7: 60–74. New York and Nashville: Abingdon-Cokesbury Press.

Robinson, J. M.
1959   *A New Quest of the Historical Jesus*. London: SCM Press.

Schmidt, K. L.
1919   *Der Rahmen der Geschichte Jesu*. Berlin: Trowitzsch.

Schweitzer, A.
1945   *The Quest of the Historical Jesus: A Critical Study of Its Progress from Reimarus to Wrede*. Translated by W. Montgomery. 2d English ed. London: A. & C. Black.

Steinmann, J.
1960   *Richard Simon et les origines de l'exegese biblique*. Paris: Desclée de Brouwer.

Sundberg, A. C.
    1975   "The Bible Canon and the Christian Doctrine of Inspiration."
                    Interpretation 27, no. 4 (1975): 352–71.
    1976   "Canon of the New Testament." In *The Interpreter's Dictionary
                    of the Bible, Supplementary Volume,* 136–40. Nashville: Abing-
                    don Press.
Tucker, G. M.
    1971   *Form Criticism of the Old Testament.* Philadelphia: Fortress
                    Press.
Wrede, W.
    1971   *The Messianic Secret.* Translated by J. C. G. Greig. Cambridge
                    and London: James Clarke & Co.

CONCLUSION

THE AIM OF this volume is to lay a foundation for understanding modern theology. The five chapters seek to clarify the challenges to traditional Christian theologies entailed in some of the major cultural revolutions that have led to the experienced world of persons living in the developed nations of the late twentieth century.

Although these explorations of natural science, philosophy, psychology, and historical biblical scholarship represent a considerable variety of subject matter, they all manifest common characteristics of the modern world, and they raise, for the most part, the same basic questions and challenges for Christian theology.

First of all, they demonstrate the fact of historical and cultural relativity, for they show that understandings, assumptions, prejudices, convictions, and concepts differ from one cultural setting to another. Most of us, upon brief reflection, realize that we would have great difficulty if we suddenly found ourselves in ancient Jerusalem or Rome or medieval Paris or London, and we are not eager to surrender the conveniences and the freedoms of our own cultural setting. Nevertheless, there are many among us today who suppose that they can continue to interpret the Christian faith in formulations that reflect the concepts and assumptions of those long-past worlds. This failure to recognize the inescapability of historical and cultural relativity is one of the more basic points of alienation between much popular Christianity today and modern theology, for that recognition is the most common characteristic of the latter. Indeed, its scholarship has shown that religion and theology have always been experienced and expressed in ways manifesting historical and cultural relativity and that Christian theology in particular has always been engaged in the process of reformulating the interpretations of its community's faith in response to cultural changes. The difference on this point between modern and premodern theologies lies in the former's clear recognition of these relativities. That recognition has been both a challenge and an opportunity for Christian theology with far-reaching implications.

Another basic challenge to Christian theology that has emerged with the development of the modern world is the concern with "how God acts" in this world. As more and more events attributed to the intervention of God in the medieval and ancient worlds have been explained by the natural and social sciences, and as knowledge of the enormities of suffering and injustice has grown, the number of persons seriously—even agonizingly—questioning God's role in the events of history and of the cosmos has been growing. Why are warfare and starvation, murder, accidents, and incurable diseases so large a part of our daily lives? What is God doing in all of this? Sooner or later such questions become terribly real for most of us.

In the midst of much disagreement about how best to answer these questions, there is growing agreement that Christian theology must address them and explore the implications of reinterpreting God's presence and will among us, even at risk of profound changes in hallowed traditional understandings.

The cultural developments reviewed in the foregoing chapters have forced upon theologians the recognition of the seriousness of "the problem of religious knowledge." In the eras in which there was little recognition of historical and cultural relativity, when the world was experienced as open to frequent incursions of various supernatural beings and powers, and when scientific method provided little if any challenge to the judgments of religious authorities, it was readily assumed that God was the source of that authority, the author of Scripture, and the guide of church teachings. Accordingly, there was little sense of a "problem of religious knowledge." *Revelation* was *assumed,* so much so that attention was rarely given to its nature and meaning.

With the emergence of the natural and social sciences, all of this has changed. Along with the growing recognition of historical and cultural relativity and of the question about how God acts, it was seen that the nature and meaning of revelation had to be examined and more carefully interpreted, if not basically reinterpreted. The recognition of the historical and human characteristics of the Scriptures made this a vital theological task. Just what we mean by "revelation," what its nature is, what its content is, what God's role is, what human response-ability is, and how the "knowledge" it provides is affected by historical and cultural relativity have been and continue to be major concerns in modern theology.

As the foregoing suggests, the development of the modern world has required the church's theologians to reexamine the issue of "authority." On what *bases* do theologians seek to answer their (and our) questions? From the beginnings of Christian theology there have been competing appeals to Scripture, tradition, church hierarchy, the voice of the Lord, and the guidance of the Holy Spirit, and there have been disagreements regarding the appropriate role of human reasoning. These debates were, however, different from the questions posed for theology by the development of the modern world. Christian theology remains dependent upon Scripture and tradition, but these are now seen to be—in significant measure—human and historical realities. We have learned things contrary to the traditional interpretations of the Scriptures authorized by church authorities, and we have gained vast amounts of useful knowledge from the sciences. It has become increasingly difficult to trust in asserted authorities that either conflict or appear to conflict with scientific learning and practical experience.

A possible implication of this last statement is that scientific learning and common everyday experience may be authorities in modern theology. If theologians are studying questions concerning the nature and meaning of revelation or the question of how God acts, should they include in a complex understanding of the bases of theological judgment such nontraditional and secular factors as these? Many in the Christian community say no, and argue for the distinctiveness of theological knowledge and its sources, norms, and authorities. It is immediately evident, however, that this is a circular argument, for it presupposes the authority of the traditional understandings of authority, revelation, and how God acts! Modern theology has grappled with the issues of authority in theology, and will continue to do so.

Along with the recognition of historical and cultural relativity and the need to reexamine the understandings of how God acts, the nature and meaning of revelation, and the factors of authority in theology, the cultural revolutions discussed above have forced the theologians to pay far closer attention to questions of language and meaning in religious discourse. These general questions have been important in some other eras of church history also, though that has usually escaped notice in the popular understandings of Christian traditions. Yet the cumulative effects of modern science in showing the inadequacy of the most basic traditional concepts (matter, cause, time, and space) and of modern depth psychologies in showing the power of the symbolic and the limits of conscious perception and reasoning in relation to meanings that most deeply affect human lives have posed the issues of language and meaning in new ways. To ask what kind of meaning is intended when we say such things as, "In the beginning God created the heavens and the earth," or what is *communicated* when we say, "I believe in God the Father almighty," is to touch but the tip of this iceberg.

This depiction of modern theology's differences from the various traditional orthodoxies and from the more widespread popular understandings of Christianity in terms of the recognition of historical and cultural relativity and the reinterpreting of how God acts, the nature and meaning of revelation, the factors of authority, and the questions of meaning in religious language should prepare readers for more fruitful study of the work of modern theologians. Yet a false impression could well be gained: the impression that modern theology is committed primarily to the authority of science and modern experience, but seeks for some unknown reason to maintain a rear-guard defense of Christian faith by removing its offensiveness to "modern ears." The character and methods of modern theology must be reflective of a primary commitment to the sovereignty of the grace of God manifest in Jesus Christ and made known to us through the witness of Scripture and tradition—the very witnesses modern theology reinterprets! In this commitment and in this task of reinterpretation modern theology is—as we now can see—essentially like the premodern theologies! This similarity and current efforts to offer answers to the questions raised by modern theology are the subject of a forthcoming volume, *Understanding Modern Theology II*.

INDEX OF
AUTHORS AND
SUBJECTS

173

INDEX OF SCRIPTURAL REFERENCES